The

Voice of History

Great Speeches of the English Language

⦿⦿⦿⦿⦿⦿⦿⦿⦿⦿⦿⦿

WITHDRAWN FROM STOCK

Iann- P bl Á

**COMHAIRLE CHONTAE ÁTHA CLIATH THEAS
SOUTH DUBLIN COUNTY LIBRARIES**

**SOUTH DUBLIN BOOKSTORE
*TO RENEW ANY ITEM TEL: 459 7834***

Items should be returned on or before the last date below. Fines,
as displayed in the Library, will be charged on overdue items.

The
Voice of History
Great Speeches of the English Language

Selected and Introduced by

LORD GEORGE-BROWN

SIDGWICK & JACKSON
LONDON

CO. DUBLIN
LIBRARY SERVICE
Acc. No. 463,057 A
Class No. 825
Cated.   Classed
Prepared
Re-bound £ 7·95
INVOICE No. 60894

First published in Great Britain in 1979
by Sidgwick and Jackson Limited

Copyright © 1979 by Lord George-Brown and Victorama Limited

The individual speeches of Baron Quickswood, the First Earl of Birkenhead, Sir Winston Churchill, Baron Carson, the First Earl Lloyd-George of Dwyfor, Arthur James Balfour, James Ramsay MacDonald, Oliver Wendell Holmes, Clarence Darrow, the First Earl Baldwin of Bewdley, President F. D. Roosevelt, Neville Chamberlain, General G. S. Patton, Aneurin Bevan, Ernest Bevin, Adlai Stevenson, President D. D. Eisenhower, Hugh Gaitskell, President J. F. Kennedy, Malcolm X, Martin Luther King Jr., Robert Kennedy and President L. B. Johnson are the copyright of the literary executors and trustees of the speakers. The speeches of Sir Oswald Mosley, Mr Harold Macmillan, President Richard Nixon and President Jimmy Carter are reproduced by kind permission of the speakers.

ISBN 0283 98521 6

Set by Ronset Limited of Darwen, Lancashire
Printed in Great Britain by
The Garden City Press Limited
Letchworth, Hertfordshire SG6 1JS

for Sidgwick and Jackson Limited
1 Tavistock Chambers, Bloomsbury Way,
London WC1A 2SG

Acknowledgements

My principal debt of gratitude must, of course, be to the one hundred or so orators whose speeches have been included in *The Voice of History*, but it would have been impossible for me to compile this selection without the assistance of diligent and resourceful researchers, chief among whom was Jennifer Browne. I am most grateful to her for all her work and for her many helpful suggestions. I am also greatly indebted to Desmond Browne, Clive Dickinson, Ben Hamilton and to my editor, Jane Heller, as well as to the staffs of the Bodleian Library, the London Library, Kensington Public Library, the United States Embassy Library, and the Research Department at Transport House.

Finally, I must thank Gyles Brandreth who originally suggested the idea of such a book to me.

Contents

The extracts appear chronologically. An alphabetical list of orators is given on p. 186.

CONTENTS

CONTENTS

CONTENTS

CONTENTS

CONTENTS

CONTENTS

INTRODUCTION

It is fashionable to remind ourselves from time to time that we are living through an epoch of technological advance greater, possibly, than has been achieved before in any comparable short period of human existence. In the past twenty-five years revolutionary means of travel and communication have shrunk the world to the point where we are as much in real as in biblical terms all neighbours of each other. It's as though the front porch of each nation has been built in the backyard of another. By the aid of satellites, events can be communicated instantaneously right across the world. Few national secrets can now be kept. It is no longer possible to keep whole peoples in ignorance of ideas, aims and achievements elsewhere, no matter how subversive or otherwise unhelpful governments or regimes may consider them.

Yet, in all this there appears to be one surprising, yet vital, casualty: the power of the spoken word to inspire or even to articulate the noble aims of men and women. It is unlikely that the spirituality of man has declined with his acquisition of greater material provision. Yet, in all of our 'developed' societies – in itself a misnomer since development cannot be a finite thing in such dynamic conditions – human ambitions for a more satisfying quality of like seem curiously muted.

This is a factor which our political leaders in the United States and in Britain are constantly bemoaning. There is said to be 'something wrong with the national mood', that 'our present-day democracies lack the will'. One constantly hears this in private conversations and at staid board room after-luncheon discussions and in the smoke rooms and corridors of our Parliaments. Certainly, I have taken part in a hundred or more such talks in the past few years at Westminster and in Washington, in New York and Baltimore, as well as in Liverpool and Birmingham.

But at the same time, and often in the very same conversations, you will hear sad tones bewailing the present-day 'absence of leaders'. The lethargy and apathetic acquiescence of people in their own exploitation and inadequacy of purpose is attributed to this total absence in our democracies over the past twenty-five years of 'real giants who could lead people'.

It is, of course, tempting to believe that this is because we are living too close to events to recognize what is actually happening. That as in the past so now only history will recognize and rescue and record those speeches which called men and women to action and so can be credited with changing or causing a particular turn in the course of events. And certainly what are now hailed as some of the epoch-making utterances of the past seem hardly to have been noticed at the time of their making. None I suppose more so than in the case of Lincoln at Gettysburg.

But, nevertheless, I find that doctrine hard to justify. And so I think will you who share with me the disability of having lived through most of this increasingly fast-moving century. It's not at all difficult to recall from one's own recollections leaders of great stature, men who have had great impact and left equally great marks on the records of our time. Politicians in the United States as diverse as the earlier Roosevelt and the Franklin D. Roosevelt of a quarter of a century later. There certainly is no doubt that for a very large part of the people of the industrialized world who lived through those terrible late twenties and early thirties the latter single-handedly restored hope and belief. They were simple appeals that he made. In times of economic crisis, social collapse, the denial of the elementary human dignities, and ultimately in time of war, his utterances were compelling and above all spelled hope and determination. And who would deny the contribution and the right of inclusion in this record of Woodrow Wilson?

In Britain during the same period there are matching figures. From Lloyd George at the beginning of the century and the opening of the new era of social and imperial change and again during the First World War when single-handedly by his words he enabled the nation to somehow survive the unsurvivable, to Winston Churchill in the 1939–45 conflict. Although any comparison of the two leaves honours even in martial terms, nothing Churchill said on social changes can compare with Lloyd George and his Limehouse speech or the later Roosevelt of the fireside chats and the New Deal. Nor were these I have mentioned alone either in America or in Britain. Readers will not find it hard to add to the list.

After 1945, however, the lists do begin to get sparse. I have been able to include a few speeches by one or two post-war figures who have succeeded in making an indelible mark, but I have had to search for those worthy of inclusion. They no longer compete in one's memory for a place. I hesitate to be adamant about the American scene, but, for myself, John F. Kennedy stands almost alone. Not only for the hundred days – the period of 'Ask not what your country can do for you; ask what you can do for your country' – but also for the 'Ich bin ein Berliner' contribution to the flagging morale of European men and women.

And so one asks why this should appear to be so. We have had playwrights and polemicists of the written word who flashed and made their mark. Even if subsequently most were consumed like meteorites by their own heat and intensity. But the zone of speech in the past twenty-five years resembles nothing so much as the terrain one crosses when leaving Cairo. The vegetation quickly disappears and what one meets is a few pathetic areas of scrub dotted by greater and greater and ultimately total aridity. Subsequently, of course, the vegetation returns and reaches great lushness as one nears Alexandria. It would be nice to think that this book by reawakening our memories and reopening the records may fulfil a similar function to that of the Nile!

To listen to speeches one must have time. The events to which they relate must have some continuity. When it all becomes just a flashing kaleidoscope one gives up. But not only for listening does one need time. The delivery – I say nothing of the composition – normally makes a similar demand. Occasionally that is not true. Again Gettysburg comes to mind – but that has to be regarded as a once for all exception to the rule. The Gettysburg Address is one of the shortest speeches in this collection and its very brevity is another feature which marks it out from the ordinary. Nowadays, one constantly meets the complaint that modern speeches are too long!

Clearly any speech – or writing for that matter – which fails to inform or entertain, to appeal to one's intellect or to one's emotion is already too long the moment that becomes apparent – after the first few minutes as validly as after a much longer period. But the complainants seldom apply that test. It so happened that just a day or so before I sat down to write this introduction the House of Lords devoted half a day's sitting to debating a motion calling for 'brevity in speeches'. Similar motions are regularly on the order paper in the House of Commons. And there is of course the benefit of an excuse for that. There are more than 600 Members of the Commons who have from time to time to get themselves re-elected. For most of them a report in a local constituency paper of something said 'in the House' is considered to give the sitting Member an advantage over a challenger who hasn't yet that possibility. Clearly the longer the time taken in any debate by some individuals the lesser the chance that others may be called upon to speak in these days of strictly limited debates. And not all local papers are willing to print the undelivered speech under the guise of a 'letter to my Constituents', or the American equivalent of something 'read into the record'. In any case the much to be desired cachet of having 'made it in the House' cannot be easily replaced. So it's almost inevitable that much of the interest of those M.P.s listening is confined to the time a speaker takes to say 'it' rather than to the quality of the manner or the value of the content of what he is saying.

Such an excuse cannot be claimed in the House of Lords however. There debates can only be closed by the Will of the House. Beyond the call of common courtesy and good manners no one is under constraint to actually listen to another. And beyond observing an orderly list to avoid chaotic and undignified competition each may speak in his turn. Yet there are those who hold that a given number of minutes should suffice for a speech rather as a given length of sheep-gut might be specified in food regulations to ensure that a housewife gets an adequate sausage. And only in the latter case is the nature of the contents felt to be a relevant matter for stipulation. However, I was more than somewhat mollified in my assessment of this particular debate by the innate good sense, understanding, and appreciation of the Noble Lord who observed that 'while many Members of your Lordships House can make three minutes seem like thirty, Lord George-Brown often speaks for thirty minutes, yet it seems no more than three'!

Faced with the scores of speeches unearthed by my diligent researchers, what criteria have I applied in making the selection that follows? Well, certainly not brevity for brevity's sake. I have tried to include speeches and short passages from speeches which have a nobility or some magic quality which instantly distinguishes them without requiring the reader or the listener to be aware of the circumstances of their delivery. Such a case in my view can be made for Erskine's defence of Thomas Payne. It stands on its own as a passionately emotive, convincing and inspiring definition of the quality of law when set against the virtuous demands of rights and reason. And even in the circumstances of today in our own land, as well as in many others, a testament of its twin bases is sadly missing. Just such another, although in a lower key, is contained in Aneurin Bevan's Commons speech at the end of the debates on the establishment of the National Health Service in 1948. It is not necessary to know that he was rebuking the professional and trade union organizations representing the doctors. What he had to say about the nature and role of a democratic nation and the rights of sectional pressure groups within it could not be more applicable to many others today.

The Aneurin Bevan inclusion raises the great problem facing anyone trying to compile in written form a collection of great oratory from great orators. The fact of the matter was put with great precision by Lord Birkett as one would expect in his essay on the Art of Advocacy where he said, 'the effect achieved depends on the character and quality of the speaker himself, the occasion on which he speaks, the subject matter of the speech, and the form in which the speech is cast'; and by Lord Chesterton when he told his son that in the case of Chatham 'his success lay more in his manner than his mouth'. The views of Birkett and Chesterton are not of course wholly consonant. For a speech to qualify as 'great' it must be a requirement that it's content shall be more than merely transient. But for Aneurin Bevan – and this can be applied to many speakers – the manner of his speech-making was so much the secret of his success that little convincing record, or indeed any record at all, actually exists of what was said. So often in the country he made tremendous orations – both as to manner and matter – but had no notes to read. It was once observed a little maliciously of a contemporary that he didn't know what he was going to say when he started and didn't know what he had said when he had finished! And he was surely no mean performer! But in Bevan's case I was always sure that the speech framework and major content was carefully prepared in his mind. The phrasing, however, came very much to mind as he proceeded. And it was this capacity for spontaneous, colourful imagery and flashing wit that so greatly distinguished him from his contemporaries. It had its dangers however. His own evident enjoyment of success in fashioning a striking phrase – always a tremendous part of his charm even when I most disagreed with what he was saying – led him into great excesses which both distorted the impact of what he was saying and left him with a great legacy of really quite unjustified misunderstanding, mistrust and even hatred. Such a case was a speech in which he used the phrase 'lower than vermin' which he was held to have applied to 'the middle classes'. In fact the allusion was always denied by those who heard it. But Bevan never escaped from it – and there's certainly no authentic record of the speech that we could have considered for inclusion in this volume. If *impact* alone be the test of a great speech, that would surely qualify it, for it was of a lasting as well as a momentary order. It might also have been included as a cautionary tale! But alas, like so much of Bevan's speaking outside of the House of Commons it was both spontaneous and recorded only in his mind. Yet there is no denying that over the period of twenty-five years his oratory had an impact as great as any and far more than most of his contemporaries on both the developing public moods and Parliamentary actions during many troubled times.

Any discussion of the methods used by different speakers in the twentieth century who qualify for inclusion in any anthology of the greats has of course to lead us to Winston Churchill. All the speeches I heard him make were highly polished, much practised performances. He was above all else an actor. He not only made the speech. He also quite carefully and deliberately made up for the part. And although one knew that, the speeches for the most part lost none of their compelling force as a result. And the apparently abbreviated notes from which he appeared to speak had the tremendous consequence of giving the living audience the feeling that he was speaking to them, and in consequence they participated in the proceedings. That he had so carefully prepared it, that the speech would be equally obviously felt by those who perforce had to rely on the written or broadcast version to be made for them, was not allowed in any way to diminish the immediate occasion. This is an art – or a technique if you prefer – that later political leaders and indeed many others who seek to communicate their views or ideas orally completely lost. Large slabs came to be read 'for the record' or 'for the T.V. cameras' so that it ended up too dull to hold the attention of either the audience present – who were no more than props – or the wider public which formed the real target. It became conventional wisdom to blame the disappearance of the live, passionately involved, often highly partisan meeting on television. In fact Winston Churchill was the great and undeniable evidence that it is no more true than most facile excuses. If an orator will try hard enough to understand his medium, address his mind to the message he wishes to impart and adapt his presentation to the circumstances of his delivery then all targets can be kept well within his range of fire.

I am often asked by interviewers to name the greatest speaker I have heard in my public lifetime. In part, for the reasons I have given above, it is a question impossible to answer. As a young man I heard Harold Laski, a leading British socialist thinker, very frequently. He broke all the rules of public speaking. Every speech was delivered as a lecture. There was the minimum of movement. As I recall, one hand on a coat lapel and one in his pocket almost throughout. Yet they were most impressive deliveries. The only failures I heard were when he went on out of character and tried to do as he was told a public speaker should. His wit, logic and orderly presentation completely took over from the physical style – which also included a dreadfully unattractive voice! I would certainly have to include him in any short list of those I have heard. But would I include Harold Macmillan? To the fury of most of my interlocutors my answer is: I would not.

There is no doubt that measured against those performing during all his later days he towered head and shoulders above them. Clearly, of all those who tried he most nearly assimilated Churchill's style – down to almost the very last mannerism. But I fear that for me the net result was to emphasize and italicize not the 'matter' but the 'manner'. And the all too evident histrionics consequently took on the character and appearance of a 'ham' acting, which led me, possibly most unfairly, to dismiss the part with the performance. But the listener whose attention is not engaged is not the one who needs to apologize. After all, his was not the initiative. However, to show how conscious I am of my minority view on this Macmillan is duly given a place in this volume. Any who read him here without ever having seen a performance will be able to judge without the disadvantage that I always felt that to be! My answer to that question posed to me must I think be either Churchill or Bevan – with a certain, but very wobbly leaning to the former!

And so I present this volume to you, with, of course, the wish that some, at least, of those chosen will give you great pleasure to read. Some may surprise, but I hope not unpleasantly. And may I offer a word of explanation, if not defence, for the frequent reliance on extracts rather than entire speeches. It was not the intention to compile an anthology of 'handy quotes'; but had I stuck to whole speeches in every instance it seemed to me that the exercise would be decidedly less valuable and much less satisfactory as an answer to the questions I particularly wished to answer. How badly off are we for leaders who can challenge, inspire or direct our thoughts, emotions and behaviour today? Has this always been so? And if not why should it now be so?

It was to find answers to these questions that I was led to compile the record. In the course of doing so I found myself almost as a by-product compiling an account which more than qualified for what would otherwise have been a much too grandiloquent title – *The Voice of History*. I believe that what follows here will seem to you, as it does to me, to be just exactly that.

To conclude on a personal, perhaps parochial, note, I can only wish that those who would have Britain seek its place in today's second division – and doubtless tomorrow's third division – had made this pilgrimage through the speeches and the thoughts of many of those who feature in these pages and who handed on to us such a high place in the *first* division. Britain was never significantly larger than now in any material respect, but she was never as limited in her ambitions as she claims now to be. From the sceptics I ask sufficient regard for the validity of their conclusions to lead them to read this book. From those who remain less than shaken I ask the patience to consult the speeches in the fuller form. For the rest I trust this volume will confirm in you, as in me, the conviction that we can still find that National role in the world that Dean Acheson asseted we lost with the liquidation of the Empire.

But above all I hope you will find as much pleasure in the reading as there was in the compilation.

Lord George-Brown
April 1979

Sir Thomas More

1478 – 1535

More entered Henry VIII's service in 1514, and until he resigned the Lord Chancellorship in 1532, when he opposed Henry's divorce, he acted on several occasions as spokesman for the King. According to Erasmus: 'His eloquent tongue so well seconds his fertile invention, that no one speaks better when suddenly called forth. His attention never languishes, his mind is always before his words, his memory has all its stock so turned into ready money, that without hesitation or delay it supplies whatever the occasion may require.'

More's speech on his installation as Lord Chancellor on 25 October 1529 illustrates the taste in oratory which then prevailed:

As for myself, I can take it no otherwise but that his Majesty's incomparable favour towards me, the good will and incredible propension of his royal mind (wherewith he hath these many years favoured me continually), hath alone, without any desert of mine at all, caused both this my new honour, and these your undeserved commendations of me; for who am I, or what is the house of my father, that the King's highness should heap upon me, by such a perpetual stream of affection, these so high honours? I am far less than any the meanest of his benefits bestowed on me; how can I then think myself worthy or fit for this so peerless dignity? I have been drawn by force, as the King's majesty often professeth, to his Highness's service, to be a courtier; but to take this dignity upon me, is most of all against my will; yet such is his Highness's benignity, such is his bounty, that he highly esteemeth the small dutifulness of his meanest subjects, and seeketh still magnificently to recompense his servants; not only such as deserve well, but even such as have but a desire to deserve well at his hands. In which number I have always wished myself to be reckoned, because I cannot challenge myself to be one of the former; which being so, you may all perceive with me, how great a burden is laid upon my back, in that I must strive in some sort with my diligence and duty to correspond with his royal benevolence, and to be answerable to that great expectation which he and you seem to have of me; wherefore those so high praises are by so much the more grievous unto me, by how much I know the greater charge I have to render myself worthy of, and the fewer means I have to make them good. This weight is hardly suitable to my weak shoulders; this honour is not correspondent to my poor deserts; it is a burthen, not glory; a care, not a dignity; the one therefore I must bear as manfully as I can, and discharge the other with as much dexterity as I shall be able. The earnest desire which I have always had, and do now acknowledge myself to have, to satisfy by all means I can possible the most ample benefits of his Highness, will greatly excite and aid me to the diligent performance of all; which I trust also I shall be more able to do, if I find all your good wills and wishes both favourable unto me, and conformable to his royal munificence; because my serious endeavours to do well, joined with your favourable acceptance, will easily procure that whatsoever is performed by me, though it be in itself but small, yet will it seem great and praiseworthy, for those things are always achieved happily which are accepted willingly; and those succeed fortunately which are received by others courteously. As you therefore do hope for great matters, and the best at my hands, so though I dare not promise any such, yet do I promise truly and affectionately to perform the best I shall be able.

In 1534 More refused to take the new oath of Supremacy to the King since it included a renunciation of all obedience to Rome. In July 1535 he was found guilty of treason in a trial held in Westminster Hall. After sentence of death was passed he spoke to the judges:

This farther only have I to say, my Lords, that like as the blessed apostle St Paul was present and consenting to the death of the protomartyr St Stephen, keeping their clothes that stoned him to death, and yet they be now twain holy saints in heaven, and there shall continue friends together for ever; so I verily trust, and shall therefore heartily pray, that, though your Lordships have been on earth my judges to condemnation, yet that we may hereafter meet in heaven merrily together to our everlasting salvation; and God preserve you all, especially my Sovereign Lord the King, and grant him faithful councillors.

On 6 July 1535 More was brought to the scaffold. He had been requested by the King not to 'use many words' at his execution, and after having pronounced the *Miserere* he contented himself with this address to his executioner:

Pluck up thy spirits, man, and be not afraid to do thine office; my neck is very short; take heed therefore thou strike not awry, for saving of thine honesty.

Bishop Hugh Latimer

?1485 – 1555

Latimer, an Anglican bishop of Worcester, was condemned to death during the religious persecution of Queen Mary's reign.

He and Nicholas Ridley, who had been Bishop of Rochester and of London, were burnt together on 16 October 1555. At the stake Latimer said to Ridley:

Be of good comfort, Master Ridley, and play the man. We shall this day light such a candle, by God's grace, in England, as, I trust, shall never be put out.

John Knox

1514 – 72

John Knox was ordained a Catholic priest in 1536, but later became a Protestant preacher and leader of the Church of Scotland. He influenced his age both as a writer and as a speaker, though he himself considered his vocation was to teach 'by tongue and lively voice in these most corrupt days rather than to compose books for the ages to come'.

On 4 April 1550 he defended his doctrine that the concept of the Mass as a sacrifice was idolatrous:

If in your Mass ye offer Jesus Christ for sin, then necessarily in your Mass must ye needs kill Jesus Christ . . . And so, Papists, if ye offer Christ in sacrifice for sin, ye shed His blood and thus newly slay Him. Advert to what fine [end] your own desire shall bring you, even to be slayers of Jesus Christ. Ye will say, ye never pretended such abomination. I dispute not what ye intended; but I only saw what absurdity doth follow upon your doctrine . . . But now will I relieve you of this anguish; dolorous it were daily to commit manslaughter, and oftentimes to crucify the King of glory. Be not afraid; ye do it not; for Jesus Christ may suffer no more, shed His blood no more, nor die no more. For that He hath died, He so died for sin, and that once; and now He liveth, and death may not prevail against Him. And so do ye not slay Christ, for no power ye have to do the same. Only ye have deceived the people, causing them to believe that ye offered Jesus Christ in sacrifice for sin in your Mass; which is frivole and false, for Jesus Christ may not be offered because He may not die.

On the death of Edward VI in July 1553 Knox feared a Catholic revival if Mary Tudor were to become Queen. When the issue between Mary and Lady Jane Grey was still undecided, Knox preached before a large congregation at Amersham. Knox later wrote an account of his sermon which he stated included the following words:

O England, now is God's wrath kindled against thee. Now hath He begun to punish, as He hath threatened a long while by His true prophets and messengers. He hath taken from thee the crown of thy glory and hath left thee without honour as a body without a head. And this appeareth to be only the beginning of sorrows, which appeareth to increase. For I perceive that the heart, the tongue and the hand of one Englishman is bent against another, and division to be in the whole realm, which is an assured sign of desolation to come. O England, England, dost thou not consider that thy commonwealth is like a ship sailing on the sea; if thy mariners and governors shall consume one another, shalt thou not suffer shipwreck in short process of time? O England, England, alas, these plagues are poured upon thee, for that thou wouldst not know the most happy time of thy gentle visitation. But wilt thou yet obey the voice of thy God, and submit thyself to His holy words? Truly, if thou wilt, thou shalt find mercy in His sight, and the estate of thy commonwealth shall be preserved. But O England, England, if thou obstinately wilt return into Egypt; that is, if thou contract marriage, confederacy or league with such princes as do maintain and advance idolatry (such as the Emperor, which is no less enemy unto Christ than ever was Nero); if for the pleasure and friendship, I say, of such princes, thou return to thine old abominations, before used under the Papistry, then assuredly, O England, thou shalt be plagued and brought to desolation, by the means of those whose favours thou seekest, and by whom thou art procured to fall from Christ and to serve Antichrist.

Queen Elizabeth I

1533 – 1603

One of the ablest of England's monarchs, Elizabeth I combined extensive learning with great flexibility of mind and quick wittedness. Formidable in audience with individuals, she was also an impressive public speaker, whether in front of experienced politicians or in front of common soldiers.

In 1566 the Commons were refusing to grant a subsidy unless the Queen settled the vexed question of who should succeed her. Elizabeth was enraged, and on 3 November she addressed thirty representatives from each House at Whitehall, asserting that no concern for the Kingdom could be greater than hers:

Was I not born in the realm? Were my parents born in any foreign country? Is there any cause I should alienate myself from being careful over this country? Is not my kingdom here? Whom have I oppressed? Whom have I enriched to other's harm? What turmoil have I made in this Commonwealth that I should be suspected to have no regard to the same? How have I governed since my reign? I will be tried by envy itself. I need not to use so many words, for my deeds do try me . . .

As for my own party, I care not for death; for all men are mortal. And though I be a woman, yet I have as good a courage, answerable to my place, as ever my father had. I am your anointed Queen. I will never be by violence constrained to do anything. I thank God I am endued with such qualities that if I were turned out of the realm in my petticoat, I were able to live in any place in Christendom.

On 9 August 1588 Elizabeth spoke words of encouragement to her soldiers at Tilbury as the Armada was sailing up the Channel:

My loving people: we have been persuaded by some that are careful of our safety to take heed how we commit ourselves to armed multitudes, for fear of treachery; but I assure you, I do not desire to live in distrust my faithful, loving people. Let tyrants fear . . . I am come among you, as you see, at this time, not for my recreation and disport, but being resolved, in the midst and heat of the battle, to live and die amongst you all . . . I know that I have the body of a weak and feeble woman, but I have the heart and stomach of a King, and of a King of England, too; and I think foul scorn that Parma, or Spain, or any prince of Europe should dare to invade the borders of my realm; to which rather than any dishonour should grow by me, I will myself take up arms, I myself will be your general, judge and rewarder of every one of your virtues in the field.

In 1601, the Commons were restless again, objecting particularly to the use of monopolies. One hundred and forty members were wooed by Elizabeth on 30 November for the last time at Whitehall. Her speech was so successful that it was known in future as the 'Golden Speech':

Mr Speaker, we perceive your coming is to present thanks to us. Know I accept them with no less joy than your loves can have desire to offer such a present, and do more esteem it than any treasure or riches; for those we know how to prize, but loyalty, love, and thanks, I account them invaluable. And though God hath raised me high, yet this I account the glory of my crown, that I have reigned with your loves. This makes me that I do not so much rejoice that God hath made me to be a Queen, as to be a Queen over so thankful a people, and to be the means under God to conserve you in safety and to preserve you from danger ... Of myself I must say this: I never was any greedy, scraping grasper, nor a strict, fast-holding prince, nor yet a waster; my heart was never set upon any worldly goods, but only for my subjects' good. What you do bestow on me, I will not hoard up, but receive it to bestow on you again; yea, my own properties I account yours, to be expended for your good, and your eyes shall see the bestowing of it for your welfare.

Lancelot Andrewes

1555 – 1626

A noted preacher who was admired by three successive monarchs, Elizabeth I, James I and Charles I, Andrewes' sermons are almost unreadable today. In one of his grandest sermons, on the 'Nativity', he said:

If this child be Immanuel, God with us, then without this child, this Immanuel, we be without God. 'Without Him in this world,' saith the apostle, and if without Him in this, without Him in the next; and if without Him then, if it be not Immanu–*el*, it will be Immanu–*hell*. What with Him? Why if we have Him we need no more; Immanu–*el* and Immanu–*all*.

John Donne

1572 – 1631

Donne had a varied career as a lawyer, a Member of Parliament and even as a soldier, before he was ordained in 1615. Throughout his life he wrote poetry, but during his last fifteen years he found a new talent – as a very successful preacher, particularly in front of sophisticated audiences at Lincoln's Inn and St Paul's Cathedral, where he became Dean in 1621. According to Izaak Walton, he was 'always preaching to himself, like an angel from a cloud, but in none, carrying some, as St Paul was, to Heaven in holy raptures, and enticing others by a sacred art and courtship to amend their lives; here picturing a vice so as to make it ugly to those that practised it, and a virtue so as to make it beloved, even by those that loved it not – and all this with a most particular grace, and unexpressible addition of comeliness . . .'

One of the earliest of his great sermons was preached on Easter Day in 1619 when he was preoccupied with his own ill health, and with the serious illness of the King:

All our life is but a going out to the place of execution, to death. Now was there ever any man seen to sleep in the cart between Newgate and Tyburn? Between the prison and the place of execution, does any man sleep? And we sleep all the way; from the womb to the grave we are never thoroughly awake; but pass on with such dreams, and imagination as these, 'I may live as well as another'; and 'Why should *I* die, rather than another?' But awake, and tell me, says this text, '*Quis homo*? Who is that other that thou talkest of? What man is he that liveth, and shall not see death?'

At St Paul's on Christmas Day 1624 he preached a sermon on God's mercies:

God made Sun and Moon to distinguish seasons, and day, and night, and we cannot have the fruits of the earth but in their seasons: But God hath made no decree to distinguish the seasons of his mercies; In paradise, the fruits were ripe, the first minute, and in heaven it is alwaies Autumne, his mercies are ever in their maturity. We ask *panem quotidianum* our daily bread, and God never sayes you should have come yesterday, he never sayes you must againe to morrow, but *to day if you will heare his voice*, today he will heare you. If some King of the earth have so large an extent of Dominion, in North and South, as that he hath Winter and Summer together in his Dominions, so large an extent East and West, as that he hath day and night together in his Dominions, much more hath God mercy and judgement together: He brought light out of darknesse, not out of a lesser light; he can bring thy Summer out of Winter, though thou have no Spring; though in the wayes of fortune, or understanding, or conscience, thou have been benighted till now, wintred and frozen, clouded and eclypsed, damped and benummed, smothered and stupified till now, now God comes to thee, not as in the dawning of the day, not as in the bud of the Spring, but as the Sun at noon to illustrate all shadowes, as the sheaves in harvest, to fill all penuries, all occasions invite his mercies, and all times are his seasons.

Sir John Eliot
1592 – 1632

Sir John Eliot's maiden speech was made in the 1624 Parliament and in March 1628 he was one of the leading supporters of the Petition of Right against Charles I and his advisers. At this time he was the House of Commons' most impassioned advocate of the rights of Parliament, claiming:

That which is more than lives, more than the lives and liberties of thousands, than all our goods, all our interests and faculties is the life, the liberty of the Parliament, the privileges and immunities of this House which are the bases and support of all the rest.

In 1632 he died in the Tower and Charles even refused permission for his body to be returned to its birthplace for burial.

Thomas Wentworth, First Earl of Strafford

1593 – 1641

Strafford, one of Charles I's principal advisers during the 1630s, was impeached by the Long Parliament of 1640. His trial opened in Westminster Hall on 22 March 1641. He spoke in his own defence, and ended with the words:

It is now full two hundred and forty years since any man was touched for this alleged crime to this height before myself. Let us not awaken those sleeping lions to our destruction, by taking up a few musty records that have lain by the walls for so many ages, forgotten or neglected.

My Lords, what is my present misfortune may be for ever yours! It is not the smallest part of my grief that not the crime of treason, but my other sins, which are exceeding many, have brought me to this bar; and, except your Lordships' wisdom provide against it, the shedding of my blood may make way for the tracing out of yours. You, your estates, your posterity, lie at the stake!

For my poor self, if it were not for your Lordships' interest, and the interest of a saint in heaven, who hath left me here two pledges on earth, I should never take the pains to keep up this ruinous cottage of mine. It is loaded with such infirmities that, in truth, I have no great pleasure to carry it about with me any longer. Nor could I ever leave it at a fitter time than this, when I hope that the better part of the world would perhaps think that by my misfortunes I have given a testimony of my integrity to my God, my King and my country. I thank God I found not the afflictions of the present life to be compared to that glory which is to be revealed in the time to come!

My Lords! my Lords! my Lords! something more I have intended to say but my voice and my spirit fail me. Only I do, in all humility and submission, cast myself down at your Lordships' feet, and desire that I may be a beacon to keep you from shipwreck.

Do not put such rocks in your own way, which no prudence, no circumspection, can eschew or satisfy, but by your utter ruin!

And so, my Lords, even so, with all tranquillity of mind, I submit myself to your decision. And whether your judgment in my case – I wish it were not the case of you all – be for life or for death, it shall be righteous in my eyes, and shall be received with a *Te Deum laudamus*, we give God the praise.

He was beheaded on 12 May 1641.

Charles I

1600 – 1649

Charles I impressed many with the speech he made on his execution day, 30 January 1649. He concluded:

What I have said so far is to show you that I am an innocent man. Now for to show you that I am a good Christian. I hope that this good man here [he pointed to Dr Juxon, Bishop of London, who was with him to the last] – will bear witness that I have forgiven all the world and even those in particular that have been the chief causes of my death. Who they are God knows. I do not desire to know. God forgive them. But this is not all. My charity must go further. I wish that they may repent, for indeed they have committed a great sin in that particular. I pray God with St Stephen that this be not laid to their charge. Nay, not only so, but that they may take the right way to the peace of the kingdom, for my charity commands me not only to forgive particular men, but my charity commands me to endeavour to the last gasp the peace of the kingdom. So, Sirs, I do wish with all my soul and I do hope that there are some here – [Charles turned towards the shorthand writers] who will carry it further that they may endeavour the peace of the kingdom . . .

For the King, the laws of the land will clearly instruct you for

11

that. Therefore, because it concerns my own particular, I only touch on it.

For the people, truly I desire their liberty and freedom as much as anybody whomsoever. But I must tell you their liberty and freedom consists in having government – those laws by which their life and their goods may be most their own. It is not having a share in government. That is nothing pertaining to them. A subject and a sovereign are clean different things and therefore, until they do that – I mean that you do put the people in that liberty as I say – certainly they will never enjoy themselves.

Sirs, it is for this that I am now come here. If I would have given way to an arbitrary power, for to have all laws changed according to the power of the sword, I need not have come here. And therefore I tell you – and I pray God it be not laid to your charge – that I am the martyr of the people.

In troth, sirs, I shall not hold you much longer. I will only say this to you – that in truth I could have desired some little time longer, because I could then have put what I have said in a little more order and a little better digested than I have done. And therefore I hope you will excuse me.

I have delivered my conscience. I pray God that you do take those courses that are best for the good of the kingdom and for your own salvations.

Oliver Cromwell
1599 – 1658

Cromwell began his career as a comparatively silent M.P. but gradually assumed a more important role as the Civil War progressed. He was an outstanding soldier, a fervently religious man and an adroit politician, and from the time of Charles I's execution until his own death he dominated English life.

Contemporary views of his oratory varied enormously. Marvell, for example, wrote of 'that powerful language' that 'charmed', whereas Burnet commented that Cromwell was famous for speaking at length and 'very ungracefully'. Certainly his famous speech to the Rump Parliament on 22 January 1654 was direct and to the point (although his exact words vary according to which contemporary account one takes):

You have sat too long here for any good you have been doing. Depart, I say, and let us have done with you. In the name of God, go!

His problems with his Parliaments were not solved with this dismissal and in February 1655 he found himself dismissing the first Parliament of his Protectorate. He himself admitted that it was 'a long speech', but it was at times picturesque:

There be some trees that will not grow under the shadows of other trees. There be some that choose (a man may say so by way of allusion) to thrive under the shadow of other trees. I will tell you what hath thriven ... instead of the peace and settlement, instead of mercy and truth being brought together, righteousness and peace kissing each other, by reconciling the honest people of these nations, and settling the woeful distempers that are amongst us ... weeds and nettles, briers and thorns, have thriven under your shadow, dissettlement and division, discontent and dissatisfaction together with real dangers to the whole.

By 1657 there were demands for the substitution of the title of King for Protector. Cromwell's attitude was equivocal. On 13 April 1657 he declared to the Commons:

For truly I have often thought that I could not tell what my business was, nor what I was in the place I stood in, save comparing myself to a good constable set to keep the peace of the parish.

Days later, he invited the House to Whitehall to hear his final reply. It could not have been more explicit:

I cannot undertake this Government with the title of King; and that is mine answer to this great and weighty business.

Jonathan Edwards

1703 – 1758

Edwards was a congregational clergyman who at Northampton, Massachusetts, led the Great Awakening. He said of his own preaching, 'The main benefit is to be by the impression made on the mind in the time of it, and not by the effect that may arise afterwards as a remembrance.'

A harsh, almost cruel, preacher, he stressed the awful punishment of hell. One Sunday in July 1741, for example, he preached a sermon at Enfield, Connecticut, which ended with the words:

If we knew that there was one person and but one, in the whole congregation, that was to be the subject of this misery, what an awful thing it would be to think of! If we knew who it was, what an awful sight would it be to see such a person! How might all the rest of the congregation lift up a lamentable and bitter cry over him! But, alas! instead of one, how many it is likely will remember this discourse in hell! And it would be a wonder if some that are now present should not be in Hell in a very short time, before this year is out. And it would be no wonder if some persons that now sit here in some seats of this meeting-house, in health and quiet and secure, *should be there before tomorrow morning.*

John Wesley

1703 – 1791

Founder of Methodism in England, Wesley's greatest strength was as an organizer. He preached throughout his life and left behind him in print 151 sermons which have been devoured by generation after generation of Methodists, and by many others. They have not, for their lasting power, depended on oratory. Wesley disliked what he termed 'fine writing' and wrote in a style that was rigorous, direct and plain. Although he admired George Whitefield as a man it is not known what he thought of him as a preacher and he certainly would not have understood Whitefield's statement that he liked to preach a sermon fifty or sixty times before he felt it was at its best.

He claimed, 'I design plain truth for plain people.' He was as good as his word.

On 25 July 1741, he preached a sermon at St Mary's, Oxford, on 'The Almost Christian'. In the second half, he questioned what was involved in being a whole-hearted or 'altogether' Christian:

. . . I answer,

(i) 1. First, the love of God. For this saith His word, 'Thou shalt love the Lord thy God with all thy heart, and with all thy soul, and with all thy mind, and with all thy strength.' Such a love [of God] is this, as engrosses the whole heart, as takes up all the affections, as fills the entire capacity of the soul, and employs the utmost extent of all its faculties. He that thus loves the Lord his God, his spirit continually 'rejoiceth in God his Saviour'. His delight is in the Lord, his Lord and his All, to whom in everything he giveth thanks. All his desire is unto God, and to the remembrances of His name. His heart is ever crying out, 'Whom have I in heaven but Thee? and there is none upon earth that I desire beside Thee.' Indeed, what can he desire beside God? Not the world, or the things of the world: for he is 'crucified to the world, and the world crucified to him'. He is crucified to 'the desire of the flesh; the desire of the eye, and the pride of life'. Yea, he is dead to pride of every kind: for 'love is not puffed up'; but 'he that dwelling in love, dwelleth in God, and God in him' is less than nothing in his own eyes.

(ii) 2. The second thing implied in the being *altogether a Christian* is, the love of our neighbour. For thus said our Lord, in the following words, 'Thou shalt love thy neighbour as thyself.' If any man ask, 'Who is my neighbour?' we reply, Every man in the world; every child of His who is the Father of the spirits of all flesh. Nor may we in any wise except our enemies, or the enemies of God and their own souls. But every Christian loveth these also as himself, yea, 'as Christ loved us'. He that would more fully understand what manner of love this is, may consider St Paul's description of it. It is 'long-suffering and kind'. It 'envieth not'. It is not rash or hasty in judging. It 'is not puffed up'; but maketh him that loves, the least, the servant, of all. Love 'doth not behave itself unseemly'; but becometh 'all things to all men'. She 'seeketh not her own'; but only the good of others, that they may be saved. 'Love is not provoked.' It casteth out wrath, which he who hath is [not made perfect] in love. 'It thinketh no evil. It rejoiceth not in iniquity, but rejoiceth in the truth. It covereth all things, believeth all things, hopeth all things, endureth all things.'

(iii) 3. There is yet one thing more that may be separately considered, though it cannot actually be separate from the preceding, which is implied in the being *altogether a Christian*; and that is the ground in all, even faith. Very excellent things are spoken of this throughout the oracles of God. 'Every one,' saith the beloved disciple, 'that believeth is born of God.' 'To as many as received Him, gave He power to become the sons of God, even to them that believe in His name.' And 'this is the victory that overcometh the world, even our faith'. Yea, our Lord Himself declares, 'He that believeth in the Son hath everlasting life; and cometh not into condemnation, but is passed from death unto life.'

4. But here let no man deceive his own soul. 'It is diligently to be noted, the faith which bringeth not forth repentance, and love, and all good works, is not that right living faith which is here spoken of, but a dead and devilish one. For even the devils believe that Christ was born of a virgin; that He wrought all kinds of miracles, declaring Himself very God; that, for our sakes, He suffered a most painful death, to redeem us from death everlasting; that He rose again the third day; that He ascended into heaven, and sitteth at the right hand of the Father, and at the end of the world shall come again to judge both the quick and dead. These articles of our faith the devils believe, and so they believe all that is written in the Old and New Testament. And yet for all this faith, they be but devils. They remain still in their damnable estate, lacking the very true Christian faith.'

5. 'The right and true Christian faith is' (to go on in the words of our own Church), 'not only to believe that Holy Scripture and the Articles of our Faith are true, but also to have a sure trust and confidence to be saved from everlasting damnation by Christ. It is a sure trust and confidence which a man hath in God, that, by the merits of Christ, his sins are forgiven, and he reconciled to the

favour of God; whereof doth follow a loving heart, to obey His commandments.'

6. Now, whosoever has this faith, which 'purifies the heart' (by the power of God, who dwelleth therein) from pride, anger, desire, 'from all unrighteousness,' from 'all filthiness of flesh and spirit'; which fills it with love stronger than death, both to God and to all mankind; love that doeth the works of God, glorying to spend and to be spent for all men and that endureth with joy not only the reproach of Christ, the being mocked, despised and hated of all men, but whatsoever the wisdom of God permits the malice of men or devils to inflict, – whosoever has this faith, thus working by love, is not almost only, but altogether a Christian.

7. But who are the living witnesses of these things? I beseech you, brethren, as in the presence of that God before whom 'hell and destruction are without a covering – how much more the hearts of the children of men?' – that each of you would ask his own heart, 'Am I of that number? Do I so far practise justice, mercy, and truth, as even the rules of heathen honesty require? If so, have I the very *outside* of a Christian? the form of godliness? Do I abstain from evil – from whatsoever is forbidden in the written Word of God? Do I, whatever good my hand findeth to do, do it with my might? Do I seriously use all the ordinances of God at all opportunities? And is all this done with a sincere design and desire to please God in all things?'

8. Are not many of you conscious that you never came thus far; that you have not been even *almost a Christian*; that you have not come up to the standard of heathen honesty; at least, not to the form of Christian godliness? – much less hath God seen sincerity in you, a real design of pleasing Him in all things. You never so much as intended to devote all your words and works, your business, studies, diversions, to His glory. You never even designed or desired, that whatsoever you did should be done 'in the name of the Lord Jesus', and as such should be 'a spiritual sacrifice, acceptable to God through Christ'.

9. But, supposing you had, do good designs and good desires make a Christian? By no means, unless they are brought to good effect. 'Hell is paved,' saith one, 'with good intentions.' The great question of all, then, still remains. Is the love of God shed abroad in your heart? Can you cry out, 'My God, and my All'? Do you

desire nothing but Him? Are you happy in God? Is He your glory, your delight, your crown of rejoicing? And is this commandment written in your heart, 'That he who loveth God love his brother also'? Do you then love your neighbour as yourself? Do you love every man, even your enemies, even the enemies of God, as your own soul? as Christ loved you? Yea, dost thou believe that Christ loved thee, and gave Himself for thee? Hast thou faith in His blood? Believest thou the Lamb of God hath taken away thy sins, and cast them as a stone into the depth of the sea? that He hath blotted out the handwriting that was against thee, taking it out of the way, nailing it to His cross? Hast thou indeed redemption through His blood, even the remission of thy sins? And doth His Spirit bear witness with thy spirit, that thou art a child of God?

10. The God and Father of our Lord Jesus Christ, who now standeth in the midst of us, knoweth, that if any man die without this faith and this love, good it were for him that he had never been born. Awake, then, thou that sleepest, and call upon thy God: call in the day when He may be found. Let Him not rest, till He make His 'goodness to pass before thee'; till He proclaim unto thee the name of the Lord, 'The Lord, the Lord God, merciful and gracious, long-suffering, and abundant in goodness and truth, keeping mercy for thousands, forgiving iniquity, and transgression, and sin.' Let no man persuade thee, by vain words, to rest short of this prize of thy high calling. But cry unto Him day and night, who, 'while we were without strength, died for the ungodly', until thou knowest in whom thou hast believed, and canst say, 'My Lord, and my God!' Remember, 'always to pray, and not to faint', till thou also canst lift up thy hand unto heaven, and declare to Him that liveth for ever and ever, 'Lord, Thou knowest all things, Thou knowest that I love Thee.'

11. May we all thus experience that it is to be, not almost only, but altogether Christians; being justified freely by His grace, through the redemption that is in Jesus; knowing we have peace with God through Jesus Christ; rejoicing in hope in the glory of God; and having the love of God shed abroad in our hearts, by the Holy Ghost given unto us!

John Wilkes

1729 – 1797

Wilkes was an M.P. and in 1762 became founder of the paper *North Briton* in which George III's court and Government were recklessly attacked. A general warrant was issued, on 26 April 1763, that those connected with issue No. 45 of the *North Briton* should be arrested, including Wilkes who, as an M.P., claimed Parliamentary privilege. On 6 May in the Court of Common Pleas, Wilkes made an impassioned speech, more to the crowd of Londoners who had packed the court than to the judges. From this date Wilkes became a popular hero and the cry 'Wilkes and Liberty!' became common.

The liberty of all peers and gentlemen, and (what touches me more sensibly) that of all the middling and inferior sets of people, who stand in most need of protection, is, in my case, this day to be decided upon . . .

Your own freeborn hearts will feel with indignation that load of oppression under which I have long laboured; close imprisonment, the effect of premeditated malice; all access to me denied; my house ransacked and plundered; every malignant insinuation, even that of high treason itself, circulated by my implacable enemies . . . Such inhuman principles of Star Chamber tyranny will, I trust, by this Court, upon this solemn occasion, be finally extirpated; and that henceforth every innocent man, however poor and unsupported, may hope to sleep in peace and security in his own house, unviolated by King's Messengers and the arbitrary mandates of an overbearing Secretary of State. I will no longer delay your justice. The nation is impatient to hear, nor can be safe or happy until that is obtained.

William Pitt, First Earl of Chatham

1708 – 1778

Pitt entered Parliament in 1735 and made an immediate impact. 'We must muzzle this terrible cornet of horse,' protested Walpole after Pitt's maiden speech. Only a few fragments of his actual speeches have been preserved, so his fame as an orator depends very much on the evidence of contemporaries, who were unanimous in their admiration. According to the Duke of Grafton, for example, he surpassed 'all that we have ever heard of the celebrated orators of Greece or Rome'. He usually spoke in general terms, without close or sustained arguments – 'more manner than matter' as Lord Chesterfield pointed out to his son.

On 14 January 1766 Pitt argued for the repeal of the notorious Stamp Act under which American colonists had been ordered to pay Stamp Duty in order to meet the cost of military defence in the New World. Fearlessly he proclaimed:

I rejoice that America has resisted. Three millions of people so dead to all the feelings of liberty as voluntarily to submit to be slaves, would have been fit instruments to make slaves of the rest.

In more detail, he set forth his view that the Americans, as British subjects and according to the British Constitution, had the right of consent to taxation for revenue:

It is my opinion that this kingdom has no right to lay a tax upon the colonies. At the same time I assert the authority of this kingdom over the colonies to be sovereign and supreme, in every circumstance of government and legislation whatsoever. They are the subjects of this kingdom, equally entitled with yourselves to all the natural rights of mankind, and the peculiar privileges of Englishmen: equally bound by its laws and equally participating of the constitution of this free country . . .

Taxation is no part of the governing power. The taxes are a

voluntary gift and grant of the Commons alone . . . when therefore in this House we give and grant, we give what is our own. But in an American tax what do we do? We your Majesty's Commons of Great Britain give and grant to your Majesty – what? Our own property? No. We give and grant to your Majesty the property of your Majesty's Commons in America. It is an absurdity in terms .

Would to God that respectable representation was augmented to a greater number! Or will you tell him [an American] that he is represented by any representative of a borough – a borough which perhaps its own representatives never saw? This is what is called 'the rotten part of the constitution'. It cannot endure the century. If it does not drop it must be amputated. The idea of a virtual representation of America in this House is the most contemptible idea that ever entered the head of man: it does not deserve a serious refutation.

On 18 November 1777 Chatham was still very much opposed to the American War and startled the House of Lords with a speech containing the famous sentence:

If I were an American, as I am an Englishman, while a foreign troop was landed in my country, I never would lay down my arms – never, never – never!

George Whitefield
1714 – 1770

Whitefield was an eighteenth-century evangelist and open-air preacher whose reputation spanned the Atlantic, and whose Georgian mission raised more money than that of Wesley. Only eighty-one of his sermons were published out of a total of 18,000, and they do not explain his phenomenal reputation as an open-air preacher. Perhaps the answer is given by David Garrick, the famous actor, who said that George Whitefield could make men either laugh or cry by pronouncing the word 'Mesopotamia'.

Some of the essence of his appeal lingers today. In one of his most famous sermons, given in Bexley Parish Church on 10 June 1739, he proclaimed:

Jesus Christ is the same, yesterday and for ever. He is the Way, the Truth, the Resurrection and the Life. Whosoever believeth on him, though he were dead yet shall he live. There is no respect of persons with Jesus Christ. High and low, rich and poor, one with another, may come to him with an humble confidence if they draw near with faith.

The love of Jesus Christ constrains me to lift up my voice like a trumpet – My heart is now full – out of the abundance of the love which I have for your immortal souls my mouth now speaketh – And I could continue till Midnight but I could speak till I could speak no more! And why should I despair of any? No, I can despair of no one when I consider Jesus Christ had mercy on such a wretch as I am.

Come then, my guilty brethren, come and believe on the Lord that bought you with his precious blood. Look up by faith and see him whom you have pierced – Behold him bleeding, panting, dying! Behold him with arms stretched out ready to receive you all – Cry unto him as the penitent thief did, Lord remember us now thou art in thy Kingdom, and he shall say to your souls, 'Shortly shall you be with me in Paradise . . .'

His very last sermon, on 29 September 1770, the night before he died, ended with the words:

I go! I go to rest prepared. My sun has arisen and by the aid of heaven has given light to many. It is now about to set – No! It is about to rise to the zenith of immortal glory!

I have outlived many on earth but they cannot outlive me in heaven. O thought divine! I shall soon be in a world where time, age, pain and sorrow are unknown. My body fails, my spirit expands. How willingly would I live for ever to preach Christ! But I die to be *with* him!

James Otis

1725 – 1783

Otis was one of the leading opponents of British rule in the years leading up to the American Revolution.

'Otis was a flame of fire!' wrote John Adams in 1817 of a speech made by Otis in 1761, but no one knows what he actually said. Doubt has even been cast on whether he ever said 'Taxation without representation is tyranny'. Like Patrick Henry, his supposed speeches were mainly the work of his nineteenth-century biographer.

Edmund Burke

1729 – 1797

An Irish political philosopher, Edmund Burke never held important political office but played a vital role in English political life of the last quarter of the eighteenth century.

As an orator, he was a paradox. He spoke indistinctly, with a strong Irish accent, and many members of the House of Commons preferred to read reports of his speeches rather than listen to him speak. Oliver Goldsmith wrote of Burke:

> *Too deep for his hearers, still went on refining*
> *And thought of convincing, while they thought of dining.*

On the other hand, the printed versions of his speeches were bought avidly, both at home and abroad.

On 19 April 1774 Burke spoke in the House of Commons on the subject of American taxation on a motion to repeal the Tea Duty:

Let us, Sir, embrace some system or other before we end this session. Do you mean to tax America and to draw a productive revenue from thence? If you do, speak out; name, fix, ascertain this revenue; settle its quantity; define its objects; provide for its collection; and then fight when you have something to fight for. If you murder, rob; if you kill, take possession: and do not appear in the character of madmen as well as assassins, violent, vindictive, bloody, and tyrannical, without an object. But may better counsels guide you!

Again and again revert to your own principles – seek peace and ensue it – leave America, if she has taxable matter in her, to tax herself. I am not here going into the distinctions of rights, not attempting to mark their boundaries. I do not enter into these metaphysical distinctions; I hate the very sound of them. Leave the Americans as they anciently stood, and these distinctions, born of our unahppy contest, will die along with it. They and we, and their and our ancestors, have been happy under that system. Let the memory of all actions in contradiction to that good old mode, on both sides, be extinguished for ever. Be content to bind America by laws of trade; you have always done it. Let this be your reason for binding their trade. Do not burthen them by taxes; you were not used to do so from the beginning. Let this be your reason for not taxing. These are the arguments of states and kingdoms. Leave the rest to the schools for there only they may be discussed with safety. But if, intemperately, unwisely, fatally, you sophisticate and poison the very source of government, by urging subtle deductions and consequences odious to those you govern, from the unlimited and illimitable nature of supreme sovereignty, you will teach them by these means to call that sovereignty itself in question. When you drive him hard, the boar will surely turn upon the hunters. If that sovereignty and their freedom cannot be reconciled, which will they take? They will cast your sovereignty in your face. Nobody will be argued into slavery. Sir, let the gentlemen on the other side call forth all their ability, let the best of them get up and tell me, what one character of liberty the Americans have, and what one brand of slavery they are free from, if they are bound in their property and industry by all the restraints you can imagine on commerce, and at the same time are made pack-horses of every tax you choose to impose, without the least share in granting them. When they bear the burthens of unlimited monopoly, will you bring them to bear the burthens of unlimited revenue too? The Englishman in America will feel that this is slavery – that it is legal slavery will be no compensation either to his feelings or his understanding.

A noble Lord [Lord Carmarthen], who spoke some time ago, is full of the fire of ingenuous youth; and when he has modelled the ideas of a lively imagination by further experience he will be an ornament to his country in either House. He has said that the Americans are our children, and how can they revolt against their parent? He says that if they are not free in their present state, England is not free, because Manchester and other considerable places are not represented. So then, because some towns in England are not represented, America is to have no representative at all. They are 'our children'; but when children ask for bread we are not to give a stone. Is it because the natural resistance of things and the various mutations of time hinder our Government, or any scheme of government, from being any more than a sort of approximation to the right, is it therefore that the colonies are to recede from it infinitely? When this child of ours wishes to assimilate to its parent and to reflect with a true filial resemblance the beauteous countenance of British liberty, are we to turn to them the shameful parts of our constitution? are we to give them our weakness for their strength? our opprobrium for their glory? and the slough of slavery, which we are not able to work off, to serve them for their freedom?

If this be the case, ask yourselves this question, Will they be content in such a state of slavery? If not, look to the consequences. Reflect how you are to govern a people who think they ought to be free and think they are not. Your scheme yields no revenue, it yields nothing but discontent, disorder, disobedience; and such is the state of America, that after wading up to your eyes in blood, you could only end just where you began; that is, to tax where no revenue is to be found, to – my voice fails me; my inclination indeed carries me no farther – all is confusion beyond it.

In a speech in the House of Commons on 22 March 1775, Burke tried to persuade the Government to conciliate the American colonies. He ended with the words:

My hold of the colonies is in the close affection which grows from common names, from kindred blood, from similar privileges, and equal protection. These are ties which, though light as air, are as strong as links of iron. Let the colonies always keep the idea of their civil rights associated with your government; they will cling and grapple to you, and no force under heaven will be of power to tear them from their allegiance. But let it be once understood that your government may be one thing and their privileges another, that these two things may exist without any mutual relation; the cement is gone, the cohesion is loosened, and everything hastens to decay and dissolution. As long as you have the wisdom to keep the sovereign authority of this country as the sanctuary of liberty, the sacred temple consecrated to our common faith, wherever the chosen race and sons of England worship freedom, they will turn their faces towards you.

The more they multiply, the more friends you will have; the more ardently they love liberty, the more perfect will be their obedience. Slavery they can have anywhere. It is a weed that grows in every soil. They may have it from Spain, they may have it from Prussia. But until you become lost to all feeling of your true interest and your natural dignity, freedom they can have from none but you. This is the commodity of price of which you have the monopoly. This is the true act of navigation which binds to you the commerce of the colonies, and through them secures to you the wealth of the world. Deny them this participation of freedom and you break that sole bond which originally made and must still preserve the unity of the empire. Do not entertain so weak an imagination as that your registers and your bonds, your affidavits and your sufferances, your cockets, and your clearances are what form the greatest securities of your commerce. Do not dream that your letters of office, and your instructions, and your suspending clauses are the things that hold together the great contexture of the mysterious whole. These things do not make your government. Dead instruments, passive tools as they are, it is the spirit of the English communion that gives all their life and efficacy to them. It is the spirit of the English constitution which, infused through the mighty mass, pervades, feeds, unites, invigorates, vivifies every part of the empire, even down to the minutest member.

Is it not the same virtue which does everything for us here in England? Do you imagine then that it is the Land Tax Act which raises your revenue, that it is the annual vote in the committee of supply which gives you your army? or that it is the Mutiny Bill which inspires it with bravery and discipline? No! surely no! It is the love of the people, it is their attachment to their government from the sense of the deep stake they have in such a glorious institution, which gives you your army and your navy, and infuses into both that liberal obedience, without which your army would be a base rabble, and your navy nothing but rotten timber.

All this, I know well enough, will sound wild and chimerical to the profane herd of those vulgar and mechanical politicians, who have no place among us; a sort of people who think that nothing exists but what is gross and material; and who, therefore, far from being qualified to be directors of the great movement of empire, are not fit to turn a wheel in the machine. But to men truly initiated and rightly taught, these ruling and master principles which, in the opinion of such men as I have mentioned, have no substantial existence, are in truth everything and all in all. Magnanimity in politics is not seldom the truest wisdom; and a great empire and little minds go ill together. If we are conscious of our situation, and glow with zeal to fill our place as becomes our station and ourselves, we ought to auspicate all our public proceedings on America with the old warning of the Church, '*Sursum corda*'. We ought to elevate our minds to the greatness of that trust to which the order of Providence has called us. By adverting to the dignity of this high calling, our ancestors have turned a savage wilderness into a glorious empire, and have made the most extensive, and the only honourable conquests, not by destroying, but by promoting the wealth, the number, the happiness of the human race.

Burke led the impeachment of Warren Hastings, a former Governor-General of India, in the proceedings which began in Westminster Hall on 13 February 1788, and lasted for seven years. Burke presented his case with the words:

I impeach Warren Hastings, Esquire, of high crimes and misdemeanours.

27

I impeach him in the name of the Commons of Great Britain in Parliament assembled, whose parliamentary trust he has betrayed.

I impeach him in the name of all the Commons of Great Britain, whose national character he has dishonoured.

I impeach him in the name of the people of India, whose laws, rights and liberties he has subverted; whose properties he has destroyed; whose country he has laid waste and desolate.

I impeach him in the name and by virtue of those eternal laws of justice which he has violated.

I impeach him in the name of human nature itself, which he has cruelly outraged, injured, and oppressed, in both sexes, in every age, rank, situation, and condition of life.

Patrick Henry
1736 – 1799

There is no doubt that Henry was a great speaker, and one of the leaders of the American Revolution. However, as his first biographer, William Wirt, wrote in a letter to a friend: '. . . from 1763 to 1789, covering all the bloom and pride of his life, not one of his speeches lives in print, writing or memory. All that is told me is, that, on such and such an occasion, he made a distinguished speech. Now to keep saying this over and over and over again, without being able to give any account of what the speech was, why, sir, what is it but a vast, open sunburnt field without one spot of shade or verdure?'

On 28 March 1775, Henry spoke before the Virginia Convention. According to one report, he ended with the words:

I have but one lamp by which my feet are guided; and that is the lamp of experience. I know of no way of judging of the future but by the past. And judging by the past, I wish to know what there has been in the conduct of the British ministry for the last ten years, to justify those hopes with which gentlemen have been pleased to solace themselves and the House? Is it that insidious smile with which our petition has been lately received? Trust it not, Sir; it will prove a snare to your feet. Suffer not yourselves to be betrayed with a kiss. Ask yourselves how this gracious reception of our petition comports with these warlike preparations which cover our waters and darken our land. Are fleets and armies necessary to a work of love and reconciliation? Have we shown ourselves so unwilling to be reconciled, that force must be called in to win back our love? Let us not deceive ourselves, Sir. These are the implements of war and subjugation; the last arguments to which kings resort. I ask gentlemen, sir, what means this martial array, if its purpose be not to force us to submission? Can gentlemen assign any other possible motives for it? Has Great Britain any enemy, in this quarter of the world, to call for all this accumulation of navies and armies? No, Sir, she has none. They are meant for us; they can be meant for no other. They are sent over to bind and rivet upon us those chains which the British ministry have been so long forging. And what have we to oppose to them? Shall we try argument? Sir, we have been trying that for the last ten years. Have we anything new to offer on the subject? Nothing. We have held the subject up in every light of which it is capable; but it has been all in vain. Shall we resort to entreaty and humble supplication? What terms shall we find which have not been already exhausted? Let us not, I beseech you, Sir, deceive ourselves longer. Sir, we have done everything that could be done, to avert the storm which is now coming on. We have petitioned; we have remonstrated; we have supplicated; we have prostrated ourselves before the throne, and have implored its interposition to arrest the tyrannical hands of the ministry and Parliament. Our petitions have been slighted; our remonstrances have produced additional violence and insult; our supplications have been disregarded; and we have been spurned, with contempt, from the foot of the throne. In vain, after these things, may we indulge the fond hope of peace and reconciliation. There is no longer any room for hope. If we wish to be free – if we mean to preserve inviolate those inestimable privileges for which we have been so long contending – if we mean not basely to abandon the noble struggle in which we have been so long engaged, and which we have pledged ourselves never to abandon until the glorious object of our contest shall be obtained, we must fight! I repeat it, Sir, we must fight! An appeal to arms and to the God of Hosts is all that is left us!

They tell us, Sir, that we are weak; unable to cope with so formidable an adversary. But when shall we be stronger? Will it be the next week, or the next year? Will it be when we are totally disarmed, and when a British guard shall be stationed in every house? Shall we gather strength by irresolution and inaction? Shall we acquire the means of effectual resistance, by lying supinely on our backs, and hugging the delusive phantom of hope, until our enemies shall have bound us hand and foot? Sir, we are not weak, if we make a proper use of the means which the God of nature hath placed in our power. Three millions of people, armed in the holy cause of liberty, and in such a country as that which we possess, are invincible by any force which our enemy can send against us. Besides, Sir, we shall not fight our battles alone. There is a just God who presides over the destinies of nations; and who will raise up friends to fight our battles for us. The battle, Sir, is not to the strong alone; it is to the vigilant, the active, the brave. Besides, Sir, we have no election. If we were base enough to desire it, it is now too late to retire from the contest. There is no retreat, but in submission and slavery! Our chains are forged! Their clanking may be heard on the plains of Boston! The war is inevitable – and let it come! I repeat it, Sir, let it come!

It is in vain, Sir, to extenuate the matter. Gentlemen may cry peace, peace – but there is no peace. The war is actually begun! The next gale that sweeps from the north will bring to our ears the clash of resounding arms! Our brethren are already in the field! Why stand we here idle? What is it that gentlemen wish? What would they have? Is life so dear, or peace so sweet, as to be purchased at the price of chains and slavery? Forbid it, Almighty God! I know not what course others may take; but as for me, give me liberty, or give me death!

Sam Adams

1722 – 1803

Adams was one of the ablest leaders of the American Revolution. He
spoke on American independence in Philadelphia on 1 August 1776:

We are now on this continent, to the astonishment of the world,
three millions of souls united in one cause. We have large armies,
well disciplined and appointed, with commanders inferior to none
in military skill, and superior in activity and zeal. We are furnished
with arsenals and stores beyond our most sanguine expectations,
and foreign nations are waiting to crown our success by their
alliances. There are instances of, I would say, an almost astonishing
Providence in our favour; our success has staggered our enemies,
and almost given faith to infidels; so we may truly say it is not our
own arm which has saved us.

The hand of Heaven appears to have led us on to be, perhaps,
humble instruments and means in the great providential dispens-
ation which is completing. We have fled from the political Sodom;
let us not look back, lest we perish and become a monument of
infamy and derision to the world. For can we ever expect more
unanimity and a better preparation for defence; more infatuation
of counsel among our enemies, and more valour and zeal among
ourselves? The same force and resistance which are sufficient to
procure us our liberties will secure us a glorious independence and
support us in the dignity of free, imperial states. We cannot
suppose that our opposition has made a corrupt and dissipated
nation more friendly to America, or created in them a greater
respect for the rights of mankind. We can, therefore, expect a
restoration and establishment of our privileges, and a compensation
for the injuries we have received, from their want of power, from
their fears, and not from their virtues. The unanimity and valour
which will effect an honourable peace can render a future contest
for our liberties unnecessary. He who has strength to chain down

the wolf is a madman if he let him loose without drawing his teeth and paring his nails.

We have no other alternative than independence, or the most ignominious and galling servitude. The legions of our enemies thicken on our plains; desolation and death mark their bloody career; whilst the mangled corpses of our countrymen seem to cry out to us as a voice from Heaven.

Our union is now complete; our constitution composed, established, and approved. You are now the guardians of your own liberties. We may justly address you, as the *decemviri* did the Romans, and say: 'Nothing that we propose can pass into a law without your consent. Be yourselves, O Americans, the authors of those laws on which your happiness depends.'

You have now in the field armies sufficient to repel the whole force of your enemies and their base and mercenary auxiliaries. The hearts of your soldiers beat high with the spirit of freedom; they are animated with the justice of their cause, and while they grasp their swords can look up to Heaven for assistance. Your adversaries are composed of wretches who laugh at the rights of humanity, who turn religion into derision, and would, for higher wages, direct their swords against their leaders or their country. Go on, then, in your generous enterprise, with gratitude to Heaven for past success, and confidence of it in the future. For my own part, I ask no greater blessing than to share with you the common danger and common glory. If I have a wish dearer to my soul than that my ashes may be mingled with those of a Warren and a Montgomery, it is that these American States may never cease to be free and independent.

Charles James Fox

1749 – 1806

A compulsive gambler, a man who lived openly with his mistress in an age of strict conventions, Fox was also a man of humanitarian principles and an influential politician, taking office on several occasions as Foreign Secretary. He led most of his life, however, in opposition to successive governments, standing as he did for the leading principles of English liberalism.

He was one of the foremost of the great eighteenth-century orators and employed a style that was natural, simple and unaffected. According to Wilberforce: 'Fox was truly wonderful. He would begin at full tear, and roll on for hours together without tiring either himself or us.'

The weaknesses of Parliamentary reporting in this era make it difficult to give a really accurate impression of Fox's speeches. In addition, Fox himself felt that a good speech lost by being set down in print and confined within the columns of newspaper or pamphlet. 'Does it read well? Then it was not a good speech' was one of his favourite sayings.

Nevertheless, the flavour of his eloquence survives in the fragments that remain.

On 26 November 1778 he attacked the war with America:

Attack France for she is your object. The nature of the war with her is quite different. The war against America is against your own countrymen; that against France is against your inveterate enemy and rival. Every blow you strike in America is against yourselves, even though you should be able, which you never will be, to force them to submit: every stroke against France is of advantage to you. The more you lower her scale, the more your own rises, and the more the Americans will be detached from her as useless to them. Even your victories over America are favourable to France, from what they cost you in men and money: your victories over France will be felt by her ally. America must be conquered in France: France never can be conquered in America.

In Westminster Hall on 2 February 1780, Fox spoke to more than 3,000 supporters of the Association movement, a body of people who were opposed to the Government of the day, and more particularly to the war against America, to high taxation and to the decline of trade.

You must be the ministers of your own deliverance, and the road to it is open . . . Your brethren in America and Ireland shew you how to act when bad men force you to feel. Are we not possessed with equal veneration for our lives and liberties? Does not the blood flow as freely in our veins as in theirs? Are we not as capable as they are of spurning at life when unaccompanied by freedom? Did not our fathers fight and bleed for their rights and transmit them as the most valuable legacy they could bequeath to posterity? . . . I trust corruption has not yet extended her debilitating influence to the people, who are the vitals of the great body politic.

In 1788 war between Russia and Turkey broke out and the Russians seized a fortress called Otchakoff in the Black Sea. Pitt at first demanded its restitution to Turkey but had to climb down after Fox's intervention with a speech made on Leap Year Day, 29 February 1792, which illustrates his debating style at its best:

If it was so important to recover Otchakoff, it is not recovered, and ministers ought to be censured. If unimportant, they ought never to have demanded it. If so unimportant, they ought to be censured for arming; but if so important as they have stated it, they ought to be censured for disarming without having gained it. Either way, therefore, the argument comes to the same point: for whether Otchakoff be, as they told us last year, the key to Constantinople, or, as they must tell us now, of no comparative importance, their conduct is equally to be condemned for disarming, and pusillanimously yielding up the object in the first instance; for committing the dignity of their sovereign, and hazarding the peace of their country, in the second. But they tell us: 'It is unfair to involve us in this dilemma; there was a middle course to be adopted. Otchakoff was certainly of much importance; but this importance was to be determined by circumstances.' Sir, we are become nice indeed in our political arithmetic. In this calculating age we ascertain to a scruple what an object is really worth. Thus it seems that Otchakoff was worth an armament, but not worth a war; it was worth a threat, but not worth carrying that threat into execution. Sir, I can conceive nothing so degrading and dishonourable as an argument such as this. To hold out a menace, without ever seriously meaning to enforce it, constitutes in common language the true description of a bully: applied to the transactions of a nation, the disgrace is deeper, and the consequences fatal to its honour ... I cannot conceive any case, in which a great nation, having committed itself by a menace, can withdraw that menace without disgrace. The converse of the proposition I can easily conceive – that there may be a case, not fit to be asked at all, but which being asked for, and with a menace, it is fit to insist upon. This undoubtedly goes to make a nation, like an individual, cautious of committing itself, because there is no ground so tender as that of honour. How do ministers think on this subject? Otchakoff was everything by itself, but when they added to Otchakoff the honour of England, it became nothing. Otchakoff, by itself, threatened the balance of Europe. Otchakoff and honour weighed nothing in the scale. Honour is, in their political arithmetic, a minus quantity, to be subtracted from the value of Otchakoff.

George Washington

1732 – 1799

The soldier-president, who hated making speeches, Washington made one of the most self-deprecating Inaugural Addresses of all time. It was delivered before the Senate on 30 April 1789, and he began:

Fellow-citizens of the Senate, and the House of Representatives: Among the vicissitudes incident to life, no event could have filled me with greater anxieties, than that of which the notification was transmitted by your order, and received on the fourteenth day of the present month. On the one hand, I was summoned by my country, whose voice I can never hear but with veneration and love, from a retreat which I had chosen with the fondest predilection, and in my flattering hopes with an immutable decision as the asylum of my declining years; a retreat which was rendered every day more necessary, as well as more dear to me, by the addition of habit to inclination, and of frequent interruptions in my health to the gradual waste committed on it by time. On the other hand, the magnitude and difficulty of the trust, to which the voice of my country called me, being sufficient to awaken in the wisest and most experienced of her citizens a distrustful scrutiny into his qualifications, could not but overwhelm with despondence, one, who inheriting inferior endowments from nature, and unpractised in the duties of civil administration, ought to be peculiarly conscious of his own deficiencies. In this conflict of emotions, all I dare aver, is, that it has been my faithful study to collect my duty from a just appreciation of every circumstance by which it might be affected. All I dare hope is, that if in executing this task, I have been too much swayed by a grateful remembrance of former instances, or by an affectionate sensibility to this transcendent proof of the confidence of my fellow-citizens, and have thence too little consulted my incapacity as well as disinclination for the weighty and untried cares before me, my error will be palliated by the motives which misled me, and its consequences be judged by my country, with some share of the partiality in which they originated.

Such being the impressions under which I have, in obedience to the public summons, repaired to the present station, it would be peculiarly improper to omit in this first official act, my fervent supplications to that Almighty Being who rules over the universe – who presides in the councils of nations – and whose providential aids can supply every human defect, that his benediction may consecrate to the liberties and happiness of the people of the United States, a government instituted by themselves for these essential purposes; and may enable every instrument, employed in its administration, to execute with success the functions allotted to his charge. In tendering this homage to the great author of every public and private good, I assure myself that it expresses your sentiments not less than my own, nor those of my fellow-citizens at large, less than either. No people can be bound to acknowledge and adore the invisible hand, which conducts the affairs of men, more than the people of the United States. Every step, by which they have advanced to the character of an independent nation, seems to have been distinguished by some token of providential agency; and in the important revolution just accomplished in the system of their united government, the tranquil deliberations and voluntary consent of so many distinct communities, from which the event has resulted, cannot be compared with the means by which most governments have been established, without some return of pious gratitude along with a humble anticipation of the future blessings which the past seems to presage. These reflections, arising out of the present crisis, have forced themselves too strongly on my mind to be suppressed. You will join with me, I trust, in thinking that there are none under the influence of which the proceedings of a new and free government can more auspiciously commence.

Henry Grattan

1746 – 1820

Henry Grattan was a member of the Irish Bar who, in 1775, became a member of the Irish Parliament. After persuading the English Parliament to remove many of the restrictions on Irish trade, Grattan aimed at legislative independence for the Irish Parliament. This he won in 1782, but it was a temporary freedom which was to end with the Act of Union in 1801.

On 19 April 1780, Grattan ended a speech in the Irish House of Commons on legislative independence for the Irish Parliament with the words:

I will not be answered by a public lie, in the shape of an amendment; neither, speaking for the subjects' freedom, am I to hear of faction. I wish for nothing but to breathe, in this our island, in common with our fellow-subjects, the air of liberty. I have no ambition, unless it be the ambition to break your chain, and contemplate your glory. I never will be satisfied so long as the meanest cottager in Ireland has a link of the British chain clanking to his rags; he may be naked, he shall not be in irons. And I do.

see the time is at hand, the spirit is gone forth, the declaration is planted; and though great men should apostatize, the cause will live; and though the public speaker should die, yet the immortal fire shall outlast the organ which conveyed it, and the breath of liberty, like the holy man, will not die with the prophet, but survive him. I shall move you, 'That the King's most excellent Majesty and the Lords and Commons of Ireland, are the only power competent to make laws to bind Ireland.'

On 26 May 1800 the Union Bill came up for its second reading in the Irish House of Commons. Grattan denounced it and ended his speech with words intended to inspire his fellow countrymen:

Yet I do not give up the country: I see her in a swoon, but she is not dead; though in her tomb she lies helpless and motionless, still there is on her lips a spirit of life and on her cheek a glow of beauty:

'Thou art not conquered; beauty's ensign yet
Is crimson in thy lips and in thy cheeks,
And death's pale flag is not advanced there.'

While a plank of the vessel sticks together, I will not leave her. Let the courtier present his flimsy sail, and carry the light barque of his faith with every new breath of wind: I will remain anchored here with fidelity to the fortunes of my country, faithful to her freedom, faithful to her fall.

Richard Brinsley Sheridan

1751 – 1816

Playwright, theatre manager and politician, Sheridan's reputation as an orator reached its height during the proceedings against Warren Hastings, a former Governor-General of India. On 7 February 1787, in the House of Commons, Sheridan moved for the adoption of the charge against Hastings concerning the Begums of Oude, the mother and grandmother of the Vizier. The Vizier had concluded a treaty with Hastings providing, among other things, that the former should take treasure rightfully belonging to the Begums and thus enable himself to repay debts to the East India Company.

The report of Sheridan's five-hour speech was meagre, though one can guess its tone from the following extract:

Great God of Justice! canst thou, from thy eternal throne, look down upon such premeditated outrages and not affix on the perpetrators some signal mark of divine displeasure!

The next year, Warren Hasting's impeachment began. On 3 June, Sheridan, as manager of the impeachment, began his speech in Westminster Hall and as much as £50 was paid for a seat. Several days later, he ended with the words:

No, my Lords, justice is not this halt and miserable object; it is not the ineffective bauble of an Indian pagod; it is not the portentous phantom of despair; it is not like any fabled monster, formed in the eclipse of reason, and found in some unhallowed grove of superstitious darkness and political dismay! No, my Lords. In the happy reverse of all this, I turn from the disgusting caricature to the real image! Justice I have now before me august and pure! The abstract idea of all that would be perfect in the spirits and the aspirings of men! – where the mind rises; where the heart expands; where the countenance is ever placid and benign; where her favourite attitude is to stoop to the unfortunate; to hear their cry and to help them; to rescue and relieve, to succour and save; majestic, from its mercy; venerable, from its utility; uplifted, without pride; firm, without obduracy; beneficent in each preference; lovely, though in her frown!

On that justice I rely – deliberate and sure, abstracted from all party purpose and political speculation; not on words, but on facts. You, my Lords, will hear me, I conjure, by those rights which it is your best privilege to preserve; by that fame which it is your best pleasure to inherit; by all those feelings which refer to the first term in the series of existence, the original compact of our nature, our controlling rank in the creation. This is the call on all to administer to truth and equity, as they would satisfy the laws and satisfy themselves, with the most exalted bliss possible or conceivable for our nature; the self-approving consciousness of virtue, when the condemnation we look for will be one of the most ample mercies accomplished for mankind since the creation of the world! My Lords, I have done.

Burke declared afterwards to the House of Commons: '. . . of all the various species of oratory, of every kind of eloquence that had been heard in ancient or modern times; whatever the acuteness of the Bar, the dignity of the Senate, or the morality of the Pulpit could furnish, had not been equal to what the House had that day heard in Westminster Hall.'

Thomas Erskine, First Baron Erskine

1750 – 1823

The greatest advocate of the French revolutionary period, Erskine took part in many of the leading cases of his day. It was a time of repression, when politicians fearing the spread of revolution sought to limit the right of free speech. One of Erskine's most famous cases was his defence of Tom Paine, who was charged with treason after the publication in 1792 of the second part of his book *The Rights of Man*. In this he had argued that all power rests ultimately with the people, that representative government should be established, and that the monarchy should be abolished. Paine was acquitted.

An extract from Erskine's defence is given below:

Gentlemen, I say, in the name of Thomas Paine, and in his words as author of *The Rights of Man*, as written in the very volume that is charged with seeking the destruction of property –

'The end of all political associations is the preservation of the rights of man, which rights are liberty, property, and security; that the nation is the source of all sovereignty derived from it; the right of property being secured and inviolable, no one ought to be deprived of it, except in cases of evident public necessity, legally ascertained, and on condition of a previous just indemnity.'

These are undoubtedly the rights of man – the rights for which all governments are established – and the only rights Mr Paine contends for; but which he thinks (no matter whether right or wrong) are better to be secured by a republican constitution than by the forms of the English government. He instructs me to admit that, when government is once constituted, no individuals, without rebellion, can withdraw their obedience from it; that all attempts to excite them to it are highly criminal for the most obvious reasons of policy and justice; that nothing short of the will of a WHOLE PEOPLE can change or affect the rule by which a nation is to be governed; and that no private opinion, however honestly inimical to the forms or substance of the law, can justify resistance to its authority, while it remains in force. The author of *The Rights of Man* not only admits the truth of all this doctrine, but he consents to be convicted, and I also consent for him, unless his work shall be found studiously and painfully to inculcate those great principles of government which it is charged to have been written to destroy.

Let me not, therefore, be suspected to be contending that it is lawful to write a book pointing out defects in the English government, and exciting individuals to destroy its sanctions, and to refuse obedience. But, on the other hand, I do contend that it is lawful to address the English nation on these momentous subjects; for had it not been for this inalienable right (thanks be to God and our fathers for establishing it!), how should we have had this constitution which we so loudly boast of? If, in the march of the human mind, no man could have gone before the establishments of the time he lived in, how could our establishment, by reiterated changes, have become what it is? If no man could have awakened the public mind to errors and abuses in our government, how could it have passed on from stage to stage, through reformation and revolution, so as to have arrived from barbarism to such a pitch of happiness and perfection, that the Attorney-General considers it as profanation to touch it further, or to look for any further amendment.

In this manner power has reasoned in every age; government, in its own estimation, has been at all times a system of perfection; but a free press has examined and detected its errors, and the people have from time to time reformed them. This freedom has alone made our government what it is; this freedom alone can preserve it; and therefore, under the banners of that freedom, today I stand up to defend Thomas Paine. But how, alas! shall this task be accomplished? How may I expect from you what human nature has not made man for the performance of? How am I to address your reasons, or ask them to pause, amidst the torrent of prejudice which has hurried away the public mind on the subject you are to judge? Gentlemen, I have but a few more words to trouble you with: take my leave of you with declaring that all this freedom which I have been endeavouring to assert is no more than the ancient freedom which belongs to our own inbred constitution. I have not asked you to acquit Thomas Paine upon any new lights, or upon any principle but that of the law, which you are sworn to administer; – my great object has been to inculcate that wisdom and policy, which are the parents of the government of Great Britain, forbid this jealous eye over her subjects; and that, on the contrary, they cry aloud in the language of the poet, adverted to by Lord Chatham on the memorable subject of America, unfortunately without effect –

> '*Be to their faults a little blind,*
> *Be to their virtues very kind,*
> *Let all their thoughts be unconfined,*
> *And clap your padlock on the mind.*'

Engage the people by their affections – convince their reason – and they will be loyal from the only principle that can make loyalty sincere, vigorous, or rational – a conviction that it is their truest interest, and that their government is for their good. Constraint is the natural parent of resistance, and a pregnant proof that reason is not on the side of those who use it. You must all remember Lucian's pleasant story: Jupiter and a countryman were walking together, conversing with great freedom and familiarity upon the subject of heaven and earth. The countryman listened with attention and acquiescence, while Jupiter turned hastily round and threatened him with his thunder. 'Ah, ah!' says the countryman, 'now, Jupiter, I know that you are wrong; you are always wrong when you appeal to your thunder.'

This is the case with me – I can reason with the people of England, but I cannot fight against the thunder of authority.

John Philpot Curran

1750 – 1817

Born and bred surrounded by the poverty of Munster and receiving his chance of schooling by the generosity of a neighbour, this ugly, stuttering man rose to eminence at the Irish Bar and became one of the greatest advocates of all time.

Curran was not a born orator. During his first case he was so overcome with nervousness that when the Chancellor asked him to speak louder, he dropped his papers and a friend had to finish the motion. Later in life he was widely held to be one of the best speakers of his day. According to Lord Byron: 'He has fifty faces and twice as many voices when he mimics . . . I have heard that man speak more poetry than I have ever seen written.'

He was so amusing at the dinner table that his servants were often unable to serve his meal as a result of laughing too much.

The 1790s were an age of repression, and Curran, as a staunch supporter of liberty of speech and of the press, undertook the defence of many accused by the State of rebellious activities. In 1794 he defended Archibald Hamilton Rowan, secretary of the Dublin Society of United Irishmen, who had published an address to the volunteers of Ireland inviting them, in view of public dangers, to resume their arms. Curran's twenty-five page speech was delivered from a few single-word notes written on the back of his brief. In one of the most famous passages, he said:

I speak in the spirit of the British law, which makes liberty commensurate with and inseparable from British soil: which proclaims even to the stranger and sojourner, the moment he sets foot upon British earth, that the ground on which he treads is holy and consecrated by the genius of universal emancipation. No matter in what language his doom may have been pronounced; no matter what complexion incompatible with freedom an Indian or an African sun may have burnt upon him; no matter in what disastrous battle his liberty may have been cloven down; no matter with what solemnities he may have been devoted upon the altar of

43

slavery; the first moment he touches the sacred soil of Britain the altar and God sink together in the dust: his soul walks abroad in her own majesty; his body swells beyond the measure of his chains, that burst from around him; and he stands, redeemed, regenerated and disenthralled by the irresistible genius of universal emancipation.

In spite of Curran's eloquence, Rowan was found guilty, fined and sentenced to two years' imprisonment. Whilst Curran was cheered home by an enthusiastic mob, Rowan was on his way to prison.

In July 1804 a Protestant clergyman, Charles Massy, accused the Marquess of Headfort of criminal conversation, i.e. of the seduction of his 24-year-old wife, who had eloped with him. The small town where the case was heard was packed with visitors and large sums were paid for a seat. After Curran's speech against the Marquess, a speech which was said to have made Queen Charlotte weep, the jury awarded Charles Massy damages of £10,000. The climax of Curran's speech came with the words:

He paraded his despicable prize in his own carriage, with his own retinue, his own servants – this veteran Paris hawked his enamoured Helen from this western quarter of the island to a seaport in the eastern, crowned with the acclamation of a senseless and grinning rabble, glorying and delighting, no doubt, in the leering and scoffing admiration of grooms and ostlers and waiters as he passed.

In this odious contempt of every personal feeling, of public opinion, of common humanity, did he parade this woman to the people, whence he transported his precious cargo to a country where her example may be less mischievous than in her own, where I agree with my learned colleague in heartily wishing he remain with her for ever. We are too poor, too simple, too unadvanced a country for the example of such achievements. When the relaxation of morals is the natural growth and consequence of the great progress of arts and wealth, it is accompanied by a refinement that makes it less gross than shocking; but for such palliations we are a century too young.

The hospitality of other countries is a matter of necessity or convention – in savage nations, of the first; in polished, of the latter; but the hospitality of an Irishman is not the running account of posted and ledgered courtesies, as in other countries; it springs, like all his qualities, his faults, his virtues, directly from his heart. The heart of an Irishman is by nature bold, and he confides; it is tender, and he loves; it is generous, and he gives; it is social, and he is hospitable. This sacrilegious intruder has profaned the religion of that sacred altar so venerable in our worship, so precious to our devotion; and it is our privilege to avenge the crime. You must either pull down the altar, and abolish the worship; or you must preserve its sanctity unabased. There is no alternative between the universal exclusion of all mankind from your threshold, and the most rigorous punishment of him who is admitted and betrays. This defendant has been so trusted, has so betrayed, and you ought to make him a most signal example.

William Wilberforce

1759 – 1833

Wilberforce sat in Parliament for nearly fifty years, and his influence was enormous. He spoke on a very wide range of subjects but is chiefly remembered for his unflagging leadership of the two great campaigns to abolish the slave trade and then to free the slaves.

On 12 May 1789, Wilberforce spoke in the House of Commons against the slave trade for the first time. He complained later of a 'a most inaccurate report' of his lengthy speech, but there was no doubt of its tremendous impact on the House.

Wilberforce summed up his position with these words:

I trust, therefore, I have shown, that upon every ground, the total abolition ought to take place. I have urged many things which are not my own leading motives for proposing it, since I have wished to show every description of gentlemen, and particularly the West-India planters, who deserve every attention, that the abolition is politic upon their own principles also. Policy, however, Sir, is not my principle, and I am not ashamed to say it. There is a principle above everything that is political; and when I reflect on the command which says, 'Thou shalt do no murder', believing the authority to be divine, how can I dare to set up any reasonings of my own against it? And, Sir, when we think of eternity, and of the future consequences of all human conduct, what is there in this life that should make any man contradict the dictates of his conscience, the principles of justice, the laws of religion, and of God. Sir, the nature and all the circumstances of this trade are now laid open to us; we can no longer plead ignorance, we cannot evade it, it is now an object placed before us, we cannot pass it; we may spurn it, we may kick it out of the way, but we cannot turn aside so as to avoid seeing it; for it is brought now so directly before our eyes, that this House must decide, and must justify to all the world, and to their own consciences, the rectitude of the grounds and principles of their decision. A society has been established for the abolition of this trade, in which dissenters, Quakers, churchmen – in which the most conscientious of all persuasions have all united, and made a common cause in this great question. Let not Parliament be the only body that is insensible to the principles of national justice. Let us make reparation to Africa, so far as we can, by establishing a trade upon true commercial principles, and we shall soon find the rectitude of our conduct rewarded, by the benefits of a regular and a growing commerce.

William Pitt the Younger
1759 – 1806

William Pitt, second son of the Earl of Chatham, became Chancellor of the Exchequer at the age of twenty-three and Prime Minister at twenty-four, in 1783. He was in office until 1801 and then again from 1804 until his death. He began office with an earnest desire for peace, but the latter part of his career was dominated by the struggle with France.

After Pitt had made his maiden speech, Burke declared that he was 'not just a chip of the old block: he is the old block itself', and the Parliamentary Register recorded: 'His voice is rich and striking, full of melody and force; his manner easy and elegant; his language beautiful and luxuriant. He gave in this first essay, a specimen of eloquence not unworthy the son of his immortal parent.'

On 2 April 1792 Pitt added his weight to the motion to end the slave trade in a speech which Fox, Grey and Windham agreed in thinking was 'one of the most extraordinary displays of eloquence' they had ever heard:

There was a time, Sir, when the very practice of the slave trade prevailed among us. Slaves, as we may read in Henry's *History of Great Britain*, were formerly an established article in our exports. 'Great numbers,' he says, 'were exported like cattle from the British coast, and were to be seen exposed for sale in the Roman market.' But it is the slavery in Africa which is now called on to furnish the alleged proofs that Africa labours under a natural incapacity for civilization; that Providence never intended her to rise above a state of barbarism; that Providence has irrecoverably doomed her to be only a nursery for slaves for us free and civilized Europeans. Allow of this principle as applied to Africa, and I should be glad to know why it might not also have been applied to ancient and uncivilized Britain? Why might not some Roman Senator, reasoning on the principles of some Hon. Gentlemen, and pointing to British barbarians, have predicted, with equal boldness, 'There is a people that will never rise to civilization; there is a people destined never to be free'? We, Sir, have long since emerged from barbarism; we have almost forgotten that we were once barbarians. There is, indeed, one thing wanting to complete the contrast and to clear us altogether from the imputation of acting even to this hour as barbarians; for we continue even to this hour a barbarous traffic in slaves.

Sir, I trust we shall no longer continue this commerce, to the destruction of every improvement on that wide continent; and shall not consider ourselves as conferring too great a boon in restoring its inhabitants to the rank of human beings. I trust we shall not think ourselves too liberal, if, by abolishing the slave trade, we give them the same common chance of civilization with other parts of the world; and that we shall now allow to Africa the opportunity – the hope – the prospect of attaining to the same blessings which we ourselves, through the favourable dispensations of Divine Providence, have been permitted, at a much more early period, to enjoy. If we listen to the voice of reason and duty, and pursue this night the line of conduct which they prescribe, some of us may live to see a reverse of that picture from which we now turn our eyes with shame and regret. We may live to behold the natives of Africa engaged in the calm occupations of industry, in the pursuits of a just and legitimate commerce. We may behold the beams of science and philosophy breaking in upon their land, which, at some happy period in still later times, may blaze with full lustre; and joining their influence to that of pure religion, may illuminate and invigorate the most distant extremities of that immense continent. Then may we hope that even Africa, though last of all the quarters of the globe, shall enjoy at length, in the evening of her days, those blessings which have descended so plentifully upon us in a much earlier period of the world. Then also will Europe, participating in her improvement and prosperity, receive an ample recompense for the tardy kindness, if kindness it can be called, of no longer hindering that continent from extricating herself out of the darkness which, in other more fortunate regions, has been so much more speedily dispelled. '*Nos . . . primus equis Oriens afflavit anhelis; Illic sera rubens accendit lumina Vesper.*'

France declared war on Britain and Holland in February 1793, and in March Pitt commented:

Many are the motives which have induced us to enter into the war. I have heard of wars of honour, and such, too, have been deemed wars of prudence and policy. On the present occasion, whatever can raise the feelings, or animate the exertions of a people, concurs to prompt us to the contest. The contempt which the French have shown for a neutrality, on our part most strictly observed; the violations of their solemn and plighted faith; their presumptuous attempts to interfere in the government of this country, and to arm our subjects against ourselves; to vilify a monarch, the object of our gratitude, reverence and affection; and to separate the Court from the people, by representing them as influenced by different motives, and acting from different interests. After provocation so wanton, so often repeated, and so highly aggravated, does not this become, on our part, a war of honour; a war necessary to assert the spirit of the nation, and the dignity of the British name? I have heard of wars undertaken for the general security of Europe; was it ever so threatened as by the progress of the French arms, and the system of ambition and aggrandizement which they have discovered? I have heard of wars for the defence of the Protestant religion; our enemies in this instance are equally the enemies of all religion -- of Lutheranism, of Calvinism; and desirous to propagate, everywhere, by the force of their arms, that system of infidelity which they avow in their principles. I have heard of wars undertaken in defence of the lawful succession; but now we fight in defence of our hereditary monarchy. We are at war with those who would destroy the whole fabric of our Constitution. When I look at these things, they afford me encouragement and consolation; and support me in discharging the painful task to which I am now called by my duty. The retrospect to that flourishing state in which we were placed previous to this war, ought to teach us to know the value of the present order of things; and to resist the malignant and envious attempts of those who would deprive us of that happiness which they despair themselves to attain. We ought to remember, that that very prosperous situation at the present crisis supplies us with the exertions, and furnishes us with the means, which our exigencies demand. In such a cause as that in which we are now engaged, I trust that our exertions will terminate only with our lives. On this ground I have brought forward the resolutions which I am now to propose; and on this ground I now trust for your support.

At the Lord Mayor's Banquet on 9 November 1805, Pitt made his last brief speech. The threat of invasion had been removed by Nelson's victory over Napoleon at Trafalgar, and the Lord Mayor proposed Pitt's health as the saviour of Europe. In reply, Pitt said:

I return you many thanks for the honour you have done me: but Europe is not to be saved by any single man. England has saved herself by her exertions, and will, as I trust, save Europe by her example.

Robert Emmet

1778 – 1803

Emmet was a young opponent of English rule over Ireland and led a hopeless rebellion in Dublin in 1803. His followers scattered, but Emmet was caught whilst trying to bid farewell to the girl he wished to marry. He was condemned to death on 19 September 1803 and hanged the following day. His speech from the dock after receiving sentence thrilled his audience. He ended with the words:

I do not fear to approach the omnipotent Judge, to answer for the conduct of my whole life; and am I to be appalled and falsified by a mere remnant of mortality here? But you, too, who if it were possible to collect all the innocent blood that you have shed in your unhallowed ministry, in one great reservoir, your Lordship might swim in it.

Let no man dare, when I am dead, to charge me with dishonour; let no man attaint my memory by believing that I could have engaged in any cause but that of my country's liberty and independence; or that I could have become the pliant minion of power in the oppression or the miseries of my countrymen. The proclamation of the Provisional Government speaks for our views; no interference can be tortured from it to countenance barbarity or debasement at home, or subjection, humiliation, or treachery from abroad; I would not have submitted to a foreign oppressor for the same reason that I would resist the foreign and domestic oppressor; in the dignity of freedom I would have fought upon the threshold of my country, and its enemy should enter only by passing over my lifeless corpse. Am I, who lived but for my country, and who have subjected myself to the dangers of the jealous and watchful oppressor, and the bondage of the grave, only to give my countrymen their rights, and my country her independence, and am I to be loaded with calumny, and not suffered to resent or repel it – no, God forbid!

If the spirits of the illustrious dead participate in the concerns and cares of those who are dear to them in this transitory life – oh, ever dear and venerated shade of my departed father, look down with scrutiny upon the conduct of your suffering son; and see if I have even for a moment deviated from those principles of morality and patriotism which it was your care to instil into my youthful mind, and for which I am now to offer up my life!

My Lords, you are impatient for the sacrifice – the blood which you seek is not congealed by the artificial terrors which surround your victim; it circulates warmly and unruffled, through the channels which God created for noble purposes, but which you are bent to destroy, for purposes so grievous, that they cry to heaven. Be yet patient! I have but a few words more to say. I am going to my cold and silent grave: my lamp of life is nearly extinguished: my race is run: the grave opens to receive me, and I sink into its bosom! I have but one request to ask at my departure from this world – it is the charity of its silence! Let no man write my epitaph: for as no man who knows my motives dare now vindicate them, let not prejudice or ignorance asperse them. Let them and me repose in obscurity and peace, and my tomb remain uninscribed, until other times, and other men, can do justice to my character; when my country takes her place among the nations of the earth, then, and not till then, let my epitaph be written. I have done.

Sir Samuel Romilly
1757 – 1818

Sir Samuel Romilly was a formidable barrister and influential Member of Parliament until his suicide in 1818, less than a week after the death of his wife. His reputation as a lawyer, a reformer and as a man was high: according to Brougham: 'Few persons have attained celebrity of name and exalted station in any country, or in any age, with such unsullied purity of character.'

In the House of Commons, he spoke clearly, concisely and simply. He himself once wrote:

... the proper eloquence of the House of Commons is plain unsophisticated reasoning expressed in forcible but familiar language, and delivered with clearness and energy but without apparent artifice or affectation. Subtlety of argument, a display of erudition, addresses to the passions, and all that the French (who have much experience of it) properly describe as the eloquence of words are not excluded indeed from the House of Commons, but are never received with approbation.

Perhaps Sir Samuel's greatest Parliamentary speech was on the second reading of the Bill to abolish the slave trade which he made on 23 February 1807. His tribute to Wilberforce at the close of this speech brought Members to their feet and even an opponent declared that it was 'as impressively eloquent perhaps as any that was ever delivered within these walls'.

What a delightful reflection it is to think that generations yet unborn will bless our memories as the authors of their liberty and happiness! But, Sir, if such will be the feelings of those who have borne any part in this transaction, or who have even witnessed its completion, what then must be the feelings of my Honourable Friend [Wilberforce]. What is there in the wide range of human ambition which could afford pleasure so pure, gratification so exalted as he must enjoy? When I look at the man at the head of the French monarchy, surrounded as he is with all the pomp of power and all the pride of victory, distributing Kingdoms to his family, and principalities to his followers, seeming, as he sits upon his throne to have reached the summit of human ambition, and the pinnacle of earthly happiness; and when I follow him into his closet, or to his bed, and contemplate the anguish with which his solitude must be tortured by the recollection of the blood he has spilt, and the oppression he has committed; and when I compare with these pangs of remorse the feelings which must accompany my Honourable Friend from this House to his home, after the vote of this night shall have accomplished the object of his humane and unceasing labours; when he shall retire into the bosom of his delighted and happy family; when he shall lay himself down upon his bed, reflecting on the innumerable voices that will be raised in every quarter of the world to bless his name; how much more enviable his lot, in the consciousness of having preserved so many millions of his fellow creatures, than that of the man, with whom I have compared him, on a throne to which he has waded through slaughter and oppression. Who will not be bound to concur with my honoured friend, in promoting the greatest act of national benefit, and securing to the Africans the greatest blessing which God has ever put it in the power of man to confer on his fellow creatures?

Daniel O'Connell

1775 – 1847

An Irish Roman Catholic political leader who sought the removal of disabilities for Catholics and repeal of the Act of Union, O'Connell was at his best during open-air political meetings rather than in the Irish or English House of Commons.
At a Catholic meeting on 29 August 1815 he said:

But we will – we must succeed. If there be an overruling Providence in heaven – if there be justice or wisdom on earth, we ought to expect success. Our liberties were not lost in any disastrous battle. Our rights were not won from us in any field of fight. No; our ancestors surrendered upon capitulation. A large army – many fortresses – a country devoted to them – foreign assistance at hand; all these our ancestors surrendered, on the faith of a solemn treaty, which stipulated, in return, for Ireland, 'liberty of conscience'. The treaty was ratified – it passed the great seal of England; it was observed – yes, it was observed by English fidelity – just seven weeks. Our claim of contract has not been worn out by time. The obligation on England is not barred by a century of injustice and oppression.
It has been attributed to the bigotry of the Catholics of Brabant and Flanders, that they have rejected the new constitution of the Netherlands, because it favoured religious liberty. Absurd calumny! They were, it is known, attached to the government of Napoleon, who established universal liberty of conscience; but there were

many and many Irish colleges and convents in Brabant and Flanders. The inhabitants had been practically informed of the breach of faith – of the violation of solemn treaty by the first Prince of Orange who reigned over Catholic Ireland. What was so natural as that they should entertain fears lest a breach of faith, a violation of treaty should signalize the first prince of that same House of Orange that was to reign over Catholic Brabant.

We are not, I repeat it, overthrown in battle. Our oppression originated in injustice. It has not been justified by any subsequent crime or delinquency on our parts. For a century and a half of sufferings, we have exhibited a fidelity unaltered and unalterable. Our allegiance to the state has been equalled only by our attachment to the faith of our fathers. But we now present the extraordinary spectacle of men at one and the same time the reproach of the justice, and the refuge and succour in danger, of the British empire. Let the hardiest of our opponents say what that empire would now be but for the Catholics of Ireland.

Thus do the Catholics urge their claims. They complain of original injustice; they insist on present merits; they require the aid of, and they place their emancipation on, the great principle of the universal right of liberty of conscience; they call on England to behold a *prelacy promoted from their superior merits, and rendering illustrious their superior station by the unobtrusive but continued exertion of all the labours and all the virtues that could ornament and dignify episcopacy.*

They call on England to behold a priesthood having no other motives but their sense of religion; seeking no other reward but the approbation of their consciences; learned, pious, and humble; always active in the discharge of their duties; teaching the young, comforting the old, instructing the ignorant, restraining the vicious, encouraging the good, discountenancing and terrifying the criminal – visiting the hovel of poverty, soothing the pangs of sickness and of sorrow, showing the path to heaven, and themselves leading the way.

They call on England to behold a people faithful even under persecution – grateful for a pittance of justice – cheerful under oppressive taxation – foremost in every battle, and giving an earnest of their allegiance and attachment to a government which they could love, by their attachment to the religion which they revere – proving, by their exclusion and sufferings, their practical reverence for the obligation of an oath; and by their anxiety to be admitted into the full enjoyment of the Constitution, how power-fully they appreciate the enjoyment of civil liberty. Such a people as this – distinguishing at one and the same time spiritual authority, which is not of this world, from temporal power, which belongs to it – giving to God the things which are God's, but preserving to Caesar the things which are Caesar's – such a nation as this, prelates, priests, and people, demand, with manly firmness, but with decent respect, their birthright – liberty, their honest earning: that which they maintain with their money, and sustain with their blood – the Constitution.

———————

Henry Peter Brougham, Baron Brougham and Vaux
1778 – 1868

A prominent barrister, Member of Parliament, and later Lord Chancellor, Brougham achieved popular fame in 1820 when he defended Queen Caroline. On his accession, George IV did not wish his wife to become Queen and determined on a divorce. A Bill of Pains and Penalties was introduced against her, a Parliamentary method of punishing a person without resort to trial in a court of law. She was accused of adultery with an Italian, Bartolommeo Pergami, and although Brougham had his doubts about the Queen's honesty ('she is pure in no sense', he said in private) he made a passionate five-hour speech in the House of Lords to open her defence (3 October 1820). According to Charles Greville it was 'the most magnificent display of argument and oratory that had been heard for years' and it moved Lord Erskine to tears.

In one of the most pathetic passages he described how the Queen had been treated on the occasion of the marriage and subsequent death of her daughter:

An event now took place which, of all others, most excites the feelings of a parent: that daughter was about to form a union upon which the happiness – upon which, alas! the Queen knew too well how much the happiness, or the misery of her future life must depend. No announcement was made to her Majesty of the projected alliance. All England occupied with the subject – Europe looking on with an interest which it certainly had in so great an event; England had it announced to her; Europe had it announced to her; each petty German prince had it announced to him; but the one person to whom no notice of it was given, was the mother of the bride who was to be espoused . . .

She heard it accidentally by a courier who was going to announce the intelligence to the Pope – that ancient, intimate, much-valued ally of the Protestant Crown of these realms, and with whose close friendship the title of the Brunswicks to our Crown is so inter-woven. A prospect grateful to the whole nation, interesting to all Europe, was now afforded, that the marriage would be a fruitful source of stability to the Royal Family of these realms. The whole of that period, painfully interesting to a parent as well as to a husband, was passed without the slightest communication; and if the Princess Charlotte's own feelings had prompted her to open one, she was in a state of anxiety of mind and of delicacy of frame, in consequence of that her first pregnancy, which made it dangerous to have maintained a struggle between power and authority on the one hand, and affection and duty on the other. An event most fatal followed, which plunged the whole of England into grief; one in which all our foreign neighbours sympathized; and while, with a due regard to the feelings of those foreign allies, and even of strange powers and princes with whom we had no alliance, that event was speedily communicated by particular messengers to each, the person in all the world who had the deepest interest in the event – the person whose feelings, above those of all the rest of mankind, were most overwhelmed and stunned by it – was left to be stunned and overwhelmed by it accidentally; as she had, by accident, heard of the marriage. But if she had not heard of the dreadful event by accident, she would, ere long, have felt it; for the decease of the Princess Charlotte was communicated to her mother by the issuing of the Milan Commission and the commence-ment of the proceedings for the third time against her character and her life.

He re-wrote the peroration seventeen times before he was satisfied with it:

Such, my Lords, is the case now before you! Such is the evidence in support of this measure – evidence inadequate to prove a debt – impotent to deprive a civil right – ridiculous to convict of the lowest offence – scandalous if brought forward to support a charge ofth e highest nature which the law knows – monstrous to ruin the honour, to blast the name of an English Queen! What shall I say, then, if this is the proof by which an act of judicial legislation, a Parliamentary sentence, an *ex post facto* law, is sought to be passed against this defenceless woman?

My Lords, I pray you to pause. I do earnestly beseech you to take heed! You are standing upon the brink of a precipice – then beware!' It will go forth your judgment, if sentence shall go against the Queen. But it will be the only judgment you ever pronounced, which instead of reaching its object, will return and bound back upon those who give it. Save the country, my Lords, from the horrors of this catastrophe – save yourselves from this peril – rescue that country, of which you are the ornaments, but in which you can flourish no longer when severed from the people, than the blossom when cut off from the roots and the stem of the tree. Save that country, that you may continue to adorn it – save the Crown, which is in jeopardy – the Aristocracy which is shaken – save the Altar, which must stagger with the blow that rends its kindred Throne! You have said, my Lords, you have willed – the Church and the King have willed – that the Queen should be deprived of its solemn service. She has instead of that solemnity, the heartfelt prayers of the people. She wants no prayers of mine. But I do here pour forth my humble supplications at the Throne of Mercy, that that mercy may be poured down upon the people, in a larger measure than the merits of its rulers may deserve, and that your hearts may be turned to justice.

George Canning

1770 – 1827

A loyal follower of Pitt, George Canning was twice Foreign Minister before becoming Prime Minister for a brief period before his death in 1827.

Formidable both in set speeches and in debate, he was said by Byron to be 'our last, our best, our only orator'. He was one of the first British politicians to be fully conscious of the importance of public opinion and tried to ensure that it was on his side. In October 1823, for example, in a speech made when presented with the freedom of the borough of Plymouth he explained why England had remained neutral when France had declared war on Spain that same year:

Let it not be said that we cultivate peace either because we fear, or because we are unprepared for war ... The resources created by peace are means of war. In cherishing these resources we but accumulate those means. Our present repose is no more a proof of inability to act, than the state of inertness and inactivity in which I have seen these mighty masses that float in the water above your town, is a proof they are devoid of strength and not fitted out for action. You well know how one of those stupendous masses, now reposing on their shadows in perfect stillness – how soon upon any call of patriotism or of necessity, it would assume the likeness of an animated thing, instinct with life – how soon it would ruffle, as it were, its swelling plumage – how quickly it would put forth its beauty and bravery, collect its scattered elements and awaken its dormant thunder. Such as is one of these mighty machines when springing from inaction into a display of its might – such is England herself, while apparently passive and motionless, she silently concentrates the power to be put forth on an adequate occasion. But God forbid that that occasion should arise.

Sometimes criticized for being no more than an actor, there was no doubt that a great deal of effort was put into each speech. Some days before each important speech Canning became feverish and anxious, and afterwards felt drained of energy.

Perhaps his most famous speech was made in the House of Commons on 12 December 1826. Again justifying Britain's non-interference in the Franco–Spanish War he pointed out that Spain had earlier been feared because of the strength of her Empire but that without that Empire she was a worthless prize. So when France occupied Spain, military intervention by Britain was unnecessary. As he declared in the House:

No, I looked another way ... I sought materials of compensation in another hemisphere. Contemplating Spain, such as our ancestors had known her, I resolved that if France had Spain, it should not be Spain 'with the Indies'. I called the New World into existence to redress the balance of the Old.

Daniel Webster

1782 – 1852

Although Daniel Webster's career as a lawyer and politician was marked with a series of frustrations, as an orator he towered over contemporaries, and some of his speeches are still learned by heart by generations of American schoolchildren.

It has been said that no man was ever as great as Daniel Webster looked with his great head, magnificent shoulders and dark brooding eyes. He spoke confidently and deliberately with a slow, musical voice, and his reputation as a speaker meant everything to him. Even on his deathbed he declared: 'Wife, children, doctor, I trust on this occasion I have said nothing unworthy of Daniel Webster.'

In Boston, August 1826, Webster made a speech in commemoration of the lives and services of John Adams and Thomas Jefferson. In a very famous passage, Webster imagined what Adams might have said when he spoke in favour of the Declaration of Independence at the Continental Congress 1776:

Sink or swim, live or die, survive or perish, I give my hand and my heart to this vote. It is true, indeed, that in the beginning, we aimed not at independence. But, 'There's a divinity that shapes our ends.' The injustice of England has driven us to arms; and, blinded to her own interest, she has obstinately persisted, till independence is now within our grasp. We have but to reach forth to it, and it is ours. Why then should we defer the declaration? Is any man so weak, as now to hope for a reconciliation with England, which shall leave either safety to the country and its liberties, or security to his own life and his own honour! Are not you, Sir, who sit in that chair, is not he [Samuel Adams] our venerable colleague, near you, are you not both already the proscribed and predestined objects of punishment and of vengeance? Cut off from all hope of royal clemency, what are you, what can you be, while the power of England remains, but *outlaws*? . . . For myself, having twelve months ago, in this place, moved you, that George Washington be appointed commander of the forces raised, or to be raised, for the defence of American liberty; may my right hand forget her cunning, and my tongue cleave to the roof of my mouth, if I hesitate or waver in the support I give him . . .

We shall make this a glorious, an immortal day. When we are in our graves, our children will honour it. They will celebrate it with thanksgiving, with festivity, with bonfires, and illuminations. On its annual return they will shed tears – copious, gushing tears; not of subjection and slavery, not of agony and distress, but of exultation, of gratitude, and of joy.

Sir, before God, I believe the hour is come. My judgment approves the measure, and my whole heart is in it. All that I have, and all that I am, and all that I hope in this life, I am now ready here to stake upon it; and I leave off as I began, that, live or die, survive or perish, I am for the declaration. It is my living sentiment, and, by the blessing of God, shall be my dying sentiment; independence *now*, and independence forever.

On 26 January 1830 Webster set out his views on Calhoun's doctrine of nullification. Calhoun had asserted that the Constitution had been established by thirteen sovereign states and that the Federal Government was merely the agent of the states. As a result, a state convention could take measures to prevent the enforcement within state limits of any Act of Congress it thought unconstitutional. Only a Federal amendment adopted by three-quarters of all the states could override the wishes of a single state.

In answer to Calhoun's spokesman, Senator Hayne, Webster spoke for hour after hour and concluded with this famous peroration:

I have not allowed myself, Sir, to look beyond the Union, to see what might lie hidden in the dark recess behind. I have not coolly weighed the chances of preserving liberty when the bonds that unite us together shall be broken asunder ... Nor could I regard him as a safe counsellor in the affairs of this Government, whose thoughts should be mainly bent on considering, not how the Union may be best preserved, but how tolerable might be the condition of the people when it should be broken up and destroyed. While the Union lasts we have high, exciting, gratifying prospects spread out before us, for us and our children. Beyond that I seek not to penetrate the veil. God grant that in my day at least that curtain may not rise! God grant that on my vision never may be opened what lies behind! When my eyes shall be turned to behold for the last time the sun in heaven, may I not see him shining on the broken and dishonoured fragments of a once glorious Union; on States dissevered, discordant, belligerent; on a land rent with civil feuds, or drenched, it may be, in fraternal blood! Let their last feeble and lingering glance rather behold the gorgeous ensign of the republic, now known and honoured throughout the earth, still full high advanced, its arms and trophies streaming in their original lustre, not a stripe erased or polluted, not a single star obscured, bearing for its motto, no such miserable interrogatory as 'What is all this worth?' nor those other words of delusion and folly, 'Liberty first and Union afterwards'; but everywhere, spread all over in characters of living light, blazing on all its ample folds, as they float over the sea and over the land, and in every wind under the whole heavens, that other sentiment, dear to every true American heart – Liberty and Union, now and forever, one and inseparable!

Thomas Babington Macaulay, First Baron Macaulay

1800 – 1859

Remembered chiefly as a writer and historian, Macaulay was also an active politician. In the House of Commons on 1 March 1831 he spoke on the Reform Bill, during which he said:

My Honourable Friend, the Member for the University of Oxford [Sir Robert Inglis] tells us that if we pass this law [extension of suffrage] England will soon be a republic. The reformed House of Commons will, according to him, before it has sat ten years, depose the King and expel the Lords from their House. Sir, if my Honourable Friend could prove this, he would have succeeded in bringing an argument for democracy infinitely stronger than any that is to be found in the works of Paine. My Honourable Friend's proposition is in fact this: that our monarchical and aristocratical institutions have no hold on the public mind of England; that these institutions are regarded with aversion by a decided majority of the middle class. This, Sir, I say, is plainly deducible from his proposition; for he tells us that the representatives of the middle class will inevitably abolish royalty and nobility within ten years; and there is surely no reason to think that the representatives of the middle class will be more inclined to a democratic revolution than their constituents. Now, Sir, if I were convinced that the great body of the middle class in England look with aversion on monarchy and aristocracy, I should be forced, much against my will, to come to this conclusion that monarchical and aristocratical institutions are unsuited to my country. Monarchy and aristocracy, valuable and useful as I think them, are still valuable and useful as means and not as ends. The end of government is the happiness of the people, and I do not conceive that, in a country like this, the happiness of the people can be promoted by a form of government in which the middle classes place no confidence, and which exists only because the middle classes have no organ by which to make their sentiments known. But, Sir, I am fully convinced that the middle classes sincerely wish to uphold the royal prerogatives and the constitutional rights of the peers.

The question of Parliamentary reform is still behind. But signs, of which it is impossible to misconceive the import, do most clearly indicate that unless that question also be speedily settled, property, and order, and all the institutions of this great monarchy, will be exposed to fearful peril; is it possible that gentlemen long versed in high political affairs can not read these signs? Is it possible that they can really believe that the representative system of England, such as it now is, will last till the year 1860. If not, for what would they have us wait? Would they have us wait merely that we may show to all the world how little we have profited from our own recent experience?

Would they have us wait, that we may once again hit the exact point where we can neither refuse with authority nor concede with grace? Would they have us wait, that the numbers of the discontented party may become larger, its demands higher, its feelings more acrimonious, its organization more complete? Would they have us wait till the whole tragicomedy of 1827 has been acted over again; till they have been brought into office by a cry of 'No Reform', to be reformers, as they were once before brought into office by a cry of 'No Popery', to be emancipated. Have they obliterated from their minds – gladly, perhaps, would some among them obliterate from their minds – the transactions of that year? And have they forgotten all the transactions of the succeeding year? Have they forgotten how the spirit of liberty in Ireland, debarred from its natural outlet, found a vent by forbidden passages? Have they forgotten how we were forced to indulge the Catholics in all the licence of rebels merely because we chose to withhold from them the liberties of subjects? Do they wait for associations more formidable than that of the Corn Exchange, for contributions larger than the Rent, for agitators more violent than those who, three years ago, divided with the King and the Parliament the sovereignty of Ireland? Do they wait for that last and most dreadful paroxysm of popular rage, for that last and most cruel test of military fidelity?

Let them wait, if their past experience shall induce them to think that any high honour or any exquisite pleasure is to be obtained by a policy like this. Let them wait, if this strange and fearful infatuation be indeed upon them, that they should not see with their eyes, or hear with their ears, or understand with their heart. But let us know our interest and our duty better. Turn where we may, within, around, the voice of greater events is proclaiming to us: Reform, that you may preserve. Now, therefore, where everything at home and abroad forebodes ruin to those who persist in a hopeless struggle against the spirit of the age; now, while the crash of the proudest throne of the continent is still resounding in our ears; now while the roof of a British palace affords an ignominious shelter to the exiled heir of forty kings; now, while we see on every side ancient institutions subverted, and great societies dissolved; now, while the heart of England is still sound; now, while old feelings and old associations retain a power and a charm which may too soon pass away; now, in this your accepted time; now, in this your day of salvation, take counsel, not of prejudice, not of a party spirit, not of the ignominious pride of a fatal consistency, but of history, of reason, of the ages which are past, of the signs of this most portentous time.

Pronounce in a manner worthy of the expectation with which this great debate has been anticipated, and of the long remembrance which it will leave behind. Renew the youth of the State. Save property, divided against itself. Save the multitude, endangered by its own ungovernable passions. Save the aristocracy, endangered by its own unpopular power. Save the greatest, and fairest, and most highly civilized community that ever existed, from calamities which may in a few days sweep away all the rich heritage of so many ages of wisdom and glory. The danger is terrible. The time is short. If this Bill should be rejected, I pray to God that none of those who concur in rejecting it may ever remember their votes with unavailing remorse, amid the wreck of laws, the confusion of ranks, the spoliation of property, and the dissolution of social order.

Andrew Jackson

1767 – 1845

Andrew Jackson, hero of the Battle of New Orleans, went on to become seventh President of the United States in 1829. During the next few years, demands for the right of any State to resist federal authority were almost overwhelming. Jackson stood firm and his catch-phrase became, 'Union men, fear not. The Union will be preserved.' Elected to a second term of office, Jackson spoke on this subject in his second Inaugural Address in March 1833:

My experience in public concerns and the observation of a life somewhat advanced confirm the opinions long since imbibed by me, that the destruction of our State governments or the annihilation of their control over the local concerns of the people would lead directly to revolution and anarchy, and finally to despotism and military domination. In proportion, therefore, as the general government encroaches upon the rights of the States, in the same proportion does it impair its own power and detract from its ability to fulfil the purposes of its creation. Solemnly impressed with these considerations, my countrymen will ever find me ready to exercise my constitutional powers in arresting measures which may directly or indirectly encroach upon the rights of the States or tend to consolidate all political power in the general government. But of equal, and, indeed, of incalculable importance is the union of these States, and the sacred duty of all to contribute to its preservation by a liberal support of the general government in the exercise of its just powers. You have been wisely admonished to 'accustom yourselves to think and speak of the Union as the palladium of your political safety and prosperity, watching for its preservation with jealous anxiety, discountenancing whatever may suggest even a suspicion that it can, in any event, be abandoned, and indignantly frowning upon the first dawning of any attempt to alienate any portion of our country from the rest, or to enfeeble the sacred ties which now link together the various parts'. Without union our independence and liberty would never have been achieved; without union they never can be maintained. Divided into twenty-four, or even a smaller number, of separate communities, we shall see our internal trade burdened with numberless restraints and exactions; communication between distant points and sections obstructed or cut off; our sons made soldiers to deluge with blood the fields they now till in peace; the mass of our people borne down and impoverished by taxes to support armies and navies, and military leaders at the head of their victorious legions becoming our lawgivers and judges. The loss of liberty, of all good government, of peace, plenty, and happiness, must inevitably follow a dissolution of the Union. In supporting it, therefore, we support all that is dear to the freeman and the philanthropist.

The time at which I stand before you is full of interest. The eyes of all nations are fixed on our republic. The event of the existing crisis will be decisive in the opinion of mankind of the practicability of our federal system of government. Great is the stake placed in our hands; great is the responsibility which must rest upon the people of the United States. Let us realize the importance of the attitude in which we stand before the world. Let us exercise forbearance and firmness. Let us extricate our country from the dangers which surround it, and learn wisdom from the lessons they inculcate.

Deeply impressed with the truth of these observations, and under the obligation of that solemn oath which I am about to take, I shall continue to exert all my faculties to maintain the just powers of the Constitution and to transmit unimpaired to posterity the blessings of our federal Union. At the same time it will be my aim to inculcate by my official acts the necessity of exercising by the general government those powers only that are clearly delegated; to encourage simplicity and economy in the expenditures of the government; to raise no more money from the people than may be requisite for these objects, and in a manner that will best promote the interests of all classes of the community and of all portions of the Union. Constantly bearing in mind that in entering into society 'individuals must give up a share of liberty to preserve the rest', it will be my desire so to discharge my duties as to foster with our brethren in all parts of the country a spirit of liberal concession and compromise, and, by reconciling our fellow citizens to those partial sacrifices which they must unavoidably make for the preservation of a greater good, to recommend our invaluable government and Union to the confidence and affections of the American people.

Finally, it is my most fervent prayer to that Almighty Being before whom I now stand, and who has kept us in His hands from the infancy of our Republic to the present day, that He will so overrule all my intentions and actions and inspire the hearts of my fellow citizens that we may be preserved from dangers of all kinds and continue for ever a united and happy people.

John C. Calhoun

1782 – 1850

A member of Congress at the age of twenty-nine, Calhoun was elected Vice-President of the United States in 1824 and again in 1828. He resigned in 1833 and returned to Congress where he preached the Southern viewpoint until his death in 1850.

According to Daniel Webster, Calhoun was 'much the ablest man in the Senate' and 'could have demolished Newton, Calvin or even John Locke as a logician'. In contrast to the other great orators of his age, content, not style, was his aim, and he spoke simply, without ornament or gestures.

On 9 March 1836, he spoke on his motion not to receive two petitions for the abolition of slavery in the District of Columbia. He argued from the premise that the sovereign states could still judge when Congress was encroaching on an individual state's power and liberty:

Our true position, that which is indispensable to our defence *here*, is that Congress has no legitimate jurisdiction over the subject of slavery either here or elsewhere. The reception of this petition surrenders this commanding position; yields the question of jurisdiction, so important to the cause of abolition and so injurious to us; compels us to sit in silence to witness the assault on our character and institutions, or to engage in an endless contest in their defence. Such a contest is beyond mortal endurance. We must in the end be humbled, degraded, broken down, and worn out.

The senators from the slave-holding States, who, most unfortunately, have committed themselves to vote for receiving these incendiary petitions, tell us that whenever the attempt shall be made to abolish slavery they will join with us to repel it . . . But I announce to them that they are now called on to redeem their pledge. *The attempt* is NOW *being made*. The work is going on daily and hourly. The war is waged not only in the most dangerous manner, but in the only manner that it can be waged. Do they expect that the abolitionists will resort to arms, and commence a crusade to liberate our slaves by force? Is this what they mean when they speak of the attempt to abolish slavery? If so, let me tell our friends of the South who differ from us that the war which the abolitionists wage against us is of a very different character, and far more effective. It is a war of religious and political fanaticism, mingled, on the part of the leaders, with ambition and the love of notoriety, and waged not against our lives, but our character. The object is to humble and debase us in our own estimation, and that of the world in general; to blast our reputation, while they overthrow our domestic institutions. This is the mode in which they are attempting abolition, with such ample means and untiring industry; and now is the time for all who are opposed to them to meet the attack. How can it be successfully met? This is the important question. There is but one way: we must meet the enemy on the frontier – on the question of receiving; we must secure that important pass – it is our Thermopylae. The power of resistance, by an universal law of nature, is on the exterior. Break through the shell, penetrate the crust, and there is no resistance within. In the present contest, the question of receiving constitutes our frontier. It is the first, the exterior question, that covers and protects all others. Let it be penetrated by receiving this petition, and not a point of resistance can be found within, as far as this government is concerned. If we cannot maintain ourselves there, we cannot on any interior position . . . There is no middle ground that is tenable.

John Henry Newman

1801 – 1890

Newman started his career as an Anglican clergyman but became a Roman Catholic in 1845 and was later made a Cardinal. He was a leader of the Oxford Movement and an extremely effective preacher.

A sermon given at St Mary's, Oxford, on the text 'Man goeth forth to his work and to his labour until the evening' ended with the words:

Oh may we ever bear in mind that we are not sent into this world to stand all day idle, but to go forth to our work and to our labour until the evening. Until the evening, not in the evening only of life, but serving God from our youth, and not waiting till our years fail us. Until the evening, not in the day-time only, lest we begin to run well, but fall away before our course is ended. Let us 'give glory to the Lord our God before He cause darkness, and before our feet stumble upon the dark mountains; and having turned to Him, let us see that our goodness be not as the morning cloud, and as the early dew which passeth away'. The end is the proof of the matter. When the sun shines, this earth pleases; but let us look towards that eventide and the cool of the day, when the Lord of the vineyard will walk amid the trees of His garden, and say unto His steward: 'Call the labourers, and give them their hire, beginning from the last unto the first.' That evening will be the trial; when the heat, and fever, and noise of the noontide are over, and the light fades, and the prospect saddens, and the shades lengthen, and the busy world is still, and 'the door shall be shut in the streets, and the daughters of music shall be brought low, and fears shall be in the way, and the almond tree shall flourish, and the grasshopper shall be a burden, and desire shall fail', and 'the pitcher shall be broken at the fountain, and the wheel broken at the cistern'; then, when it is 'vanity of vanities, all is vanity', and the Lord shall come, 'who both will bring to light the hidden things of darkness, and will make manifest the counsels of the hearts'; then shall we 'discern between the righteous and the wicked, between him that serveth God and him that serveth Him not'.

May the day and that hour ever be in our thoughts, when we rise, when we lie down; when we speak, when we are silent; when we act, and when we rest: whether we eat or drink, or whatever we do, may we never forget that 'for all these things God will bring us into judgment!' For 'He cometh quickly, and His reward is with Him, to give every man according to His work shall be.'

'Blessed are they that do His Commandments, that they may have right to the tree of life, and may enter in through the gates into the city.' Blessed will they be then, and only they, who, with the Apostle, have ever had on their lips, and in their hearts, the question, 'Lord what wilt Thou have me to do?' whose soul, 'hath broken out for the very fervent desire that it hath alway unto His judgments'; who have 'made haste and prolonged not the time to keep His Commandments'; who have not waited to be hired, nor run uncertainly, nor beaten the air, nor taken darkness for light, and light for darkness, nor contented themselves with knowing what is right, nor taken comfort in feeling what is good, nor prided themselves in their privileges, but set themselves vigorously to do God's will.

Let us turn from shadows of all kinds – shadows of sense, or shadows of argument and disputation, or shadows addressed to our imagination and tastes. Let us attempt, through God's grace, to advance and sanctify the inward man. We cannot be wrong here. Whatever is right, whatever is wrong, in this perplexing world, we must be right in doing justly, in living mercy, in walking humbly with our God; in denying our wills, in ruling our tongues, in softening and sweetening our tempers, in mortifying our lusts; in learning patience, meekness, purity, forgiveness of injuries, and continuance in well-doing.

Brigham Young

1801 – 1877

Young became the leader of the Mormon sect on Joseph Smith's death, and subsequently marched his followers to central Utah where he directed the establishment of over three hundred towns, and built railroads, stores and factories.

In 1840 he came to England for a year, during which period he baptised between eight and nine thousand people. His success as a speaker depended as much on the emotional susceptibilities of his audience as on his own ability. An observer at a meeting found himself 'in the midst of shoutings, wailing, fallings, contortions, trances, visions, speaking in unknown tongues, and prophesying that require the pen of a Trollope to describe'. Still, he was an impressive speaker, as the *New York Herald* reported in 1858: 'His articulation was very distinct; every syllable could be heard. His gesticulations were not elaborate or constant, but strong and impressive. His style of elocution was not so winning as commanding, though he by no means lacks suavity . . . He uses whatever word comes first to express his idea, so his language is quite original and his expressions frequently very telling. His language does not flow along like a torrent, but is strong, harsh and commanding . . . He could not minister to a graceful and accomplished society, but he is a man preeminently qualified to rule a mountain people with a rod of iron and a gloved hand.'

On 8 August 1844 Young made possibly the most famous speech in Mormon history. A number of candidates were presenting their claims to leadership of the Mormon church, and Young put in his bid:

If the people want President Rigdon to lead them they may have him; but I say unto you that the Quorum of the Twelve have the keys of the kingdom of God in all the world. The Twelve are appointed by the finger of God. Here is Brigham, have his knees ever faltered? have his lips ever quivered? Here is Heber and the rest of the Twelve, an independent body, who have the keys of the Priesthood – the keys of the kingdom of God to deliver to all the world: this is true, so help me God. They stand next to Joseph, and are as the First Presidency of the Church . . . You cannot fill the office of a Prophet, Seer and Revelator: God must do this. You are like children without a father and sheep without a shepherd. You must not appoint any man at our head; if you should, the Twelve must ordain him. You cannot appoint a man at our head; but if you do want any other man or men to lead you, take them and we will go our way to build up the kingdom in all the world.

It later became a Mormon legend that Young made this speech with the voice and appearance of Joseph Smith.

Richard Cobden

1804 – 1865

Richard Cobden was a leading nineteenth-century radical who, with John Bright, directed the movement against the Corn Laws. Cobden was a powerful speaker. On 13 March 1845, he bitterly attacked the Corn Laws. Sir Robert Peel is said to have said: 'You may answer this, for I cannot.'
The speech ended thus:

With mere politicians I have no right to expect to succeed in this motion. But I have no hesitation in telling you that, if you give me a committee of this House, I will explode the delusion of agricultural protection! I will bring forward such a mass of evidence, and give you such a preponderance of talent and of authority, that when the blue book is published and sent forth to the world, as we can now send it, by our vehicles of information, your system of protection shall not live in public opinion for two years afterward. Politicians do not want that. This cry of protection has been a very convenient handle for politicians. The cry of protection carried the counties at the last election, and politicians gained honours, emoluments, and place by it. But is that old tattered flag of protection, tarnished and torn as it is already, to be kept hoisted still in the counties for the benefit of politicians; or will you come forward honestly and fairly to inquire into this question? I cannot believe that the gentry of England will be made mere drumheads to be sounded upon by a Prime Minister, to give forth unmeaning and empty sounds, and to have no articulate voice of their own. No! You are the gentry of England who represent the counties. You are the aristocracy of England. Your fathers led our fathers; you may lead us if you will go the right way. But, although you have retained your influence with this country longer than any other aristocracy, it has not been by opposing popular opinion, or by setting yourselves against the spirit of the age.

In other days, when the battle and the hunting-fields were the tests of manly vigour, your fathers were first and foremost there. The aristocracy of England were not like the noblesse of France, the mere minions of a court; nor were they like the hidalgos of Madrid, who dwindled into pigmies. You have been Englishmen. You have not shown a want of courage and firmness when any call has been made upon you. This is a new era. It is the age of improvement; it is the age of social advancement, not the age for war or for feudal sports. You live in a mercantile age, when the whole wealth of the world is poured into your lap. You cannot have the advantages of commercial rents and feudal privileges; but you may be what you always have been, if you will identify yourselves with the spirit of the age. The English people look to the gentry and aristocracy of their country as their leaders. I, who am not one of you, have no hesitation in telling you that there is a deep-rooted, an hereditary prejudice, if I may so call it, in your favour in this country. But you never got it, and you will not keep it, by obstructing the spirit of the age. If you are indifferent to enlightened means of finding employment for your own peasantry; if you are found obstructing that advance which is calculated to knit nations more together in the bonds of peace by means of commercial intercourse; if you are found fighting against the discoveries which have almost given breath and life to material nature, and setting up yourselves as obstructives of that which destiny has decreed shall go on – why, then, you will be the gentry of England no longer, and others will be found to take your place.

And I have no hesitation in saying that you stand just now in a very critical position. There is a wide-spread suspicion that you have been tampering with the best feelings and with the honest confidence of your constituents in this cause. Everywhere you are doubted and suspected. Read your own organs, and you will see that this is the case. Well, then, this is the time to show that you are not the mere party politicians which you are said to be. I have said that we shall be opposed in this measure by politicians; they do not want inquiry. But I ask you to go into this committee with me. I will give you a majority of county members. You shall have a majority of the Central Society in that committee. I ask you only to go into a fair inquiry as to the causes of the distress of your own population. I only ask that this matter may be fairly examined. Whether you establish my principle or yours, good will come out of the inquiry; and I do, therefore, beg and entreat the honourable independent country gentlemen of this House that they will not refuse, on this occasion, to go into a fair, a full, and an impartial inquiry.

Benjamin Disraeli, First Earl of Beaconsfield
1804 – 1881

Disraeli's maiden speech in the House of Commons was a complete failure. He had to sit down, his voice drowned by an uproar, but before he did, he shouted: 'I will sit down now, but the time will come when you will hear me.'

He lived up to this claim, breaking Sir Robert Peel as Tory party leader and later moulding the Tory party into new shape both in Opposition and during his premiership from 1874 to 1880.

On 11 April 1845 Peel, as Prime Minister, proposed greatly increasing the Government grant to the Maynooth seminary in Ireland for the education of Catholic priests. In a biting speech, delivered without notes, Disraeli opposed the suggestion. His attitude was indefensible but he was really aiming another attack on Peel as party leader.

If you are to have a popular Government – if you are to have a Parliamentary administration the conditions antecedent are, that you should have a government which declares the principles upon which its policy is founded, and then you can have the wholesome check of a constitutional Opposition. What have we got instead? Something has risen up in this country as fatal in the political world, as it has been in the landed world of Ireland – we have a great Parliamentary middleman. It is well known what a middleman is; he is a man who bamboozles one party and plunders the other, till, having obtained a position to which he is not entitled, he cries out, 'Let us have no party questions, but fixity of tenure.' I want to have a Commission issued to inquire into the tenure by which Downing Street is held ... I hope I shall not be answered by *Hansard* [Peel's speech had been full of quotations from *Hansard*] ... What dreary pages of interminable talk, what predictions falsified, what pledges broken, what calculations that have gone wrong, what budgets that have blown up! And all this too, not relieved by a single original thought, a single generous impulse, or a single happy expression! Why *Hansard*, instead of being the Delphi of Downing Street is but the Dunciad of politics ...

Let us in this House re-echo that which I believe to be the sovereign sentiment of this country; let us tell persons in high places that cunning is not caution, and that habitual perfidy is not high policy of State. On that ground we may all join. Let us bring back to this House that which it has for so long a time past been without – the legitimate influence and salutary check of a constitutional Opposition. Let us do it at once in the only way in which it can be done, by dethroning this dynasty of deception, by putting an end to the intolerable yoke of official despotism and Parliamentary imposture.

On 27 June 1878 Disraeli spoke at a banquet given in his honour at the Mansion House, London, after his triumphal return from the Congress of Berlin:

When I study the catalogue of congratulatory regrets with attention, the Convention of Constantinople appears to be the ground on which a great assault is to be made on the government. It is said that we have increased, and dangerously increased, our responsibilities as a nation by that Convention. In the first place, I deny that we have increased our responsibilities by that Convention. I maintain that by that Convention we have lessened our responsibilities. Suppose now, for example, the settlement of Europe had not included the Convention of Constantinople and the occupation of the isle of Cyprus; suppose it had been limited to the mere

75

Treaty of Berlin; what, under all probable circumstances, might then have occurred? In ten, fifteen, it might be in twenty, years, the power and resources of Russia having revived, some quarrel would again have occurred, Bulgarian or otherwise, and in all probability the armies of Russia would have been assailing the Ottoman dominions both in Europe and Asia, and enveloping and enclosing the city of Constantinople and its all-powerful position.

Now, what would be the probable conduct, under these circumstances, of the Government of this country, whoever the ministers might be, whatever party might be in power? I fear there might be hesitation for a time – a want of decision – a want of firmness; but no one doubts that ultimately England would have said: 'This will never do; we must prevent the conquest of Asia Minor; we must interfere in this matter, and arrest the course of Russia.' No one, I am sure, in this country who impartially considers the question can for a moment doubt what, under any circumstances, would have been the course of this country.

Well, then, that being the case, I say it is extremely important that this country should take a step beforehand which should indicate what the policy of England would be; that you should not have your ministers meeting in a Council Chamber, hesitating and doubting and considering contingencies, and then acting at last, but perhaps acting too late. I say, therefore, that the responsibilities of this country have not been increased; the responsibilities already existed, though I for one would never shrink from increasing the responsibilities of this country, if they are responsibilities which ought to be undertaken. The responsibilities of this country are practically diminished by the course we have taken.

My Lords and Gentlemen, one of the results of my attending the Congress of Berlin has been to prove, what I always suspected to be the absolute fact, that neither the Crimean War, nor this horrible devastating war which has just terminated, would have taken place, if England had spoken with the necessary firmness.

Russia has complaints to make against this country that neither in the case of the Crimean War nor on this occasion – and I do not shrink from my share of the responsibility in this matter – was the voice of England so clear and decided as to exercise a due share in the guidance of European opinion.

Suppose, gentlemen, that my noble friend and I had come back with the Treaty of Berlin, and had not taken the step which is to be questioned within the next eight-and-forty hours, could we with any self-respect, have met our countrymen when they asked, what securities have you made for the peace of Europe? How far have you diminished the chance of perpetually recurring war on this question of the East by the Treaty of Berlin? Why, they could say, all we have gained by the Treaty of Berlin is probably the peace of a few years, and at the end of that time the same phenomenon will arise and the Ministers of England must patch up the affair as well as they could.

That was not the idea of public duty entertained by my noble friend and myself. We thought the time had come when we ought to take steps which would produce some order out of the anarchy and chaos that had so long prevailed. We asked ourselves, was it absolutely a necessity that the fairest provinces of the world should be the most devastated and most ill-used, and for this reason that there is no security for life or property so long as that country is in perpetual fear of invasion and aggression?

It was under these circumstances that we recommended the course we have taken; and I believe that the consequences of that policy will tend to and even secure peace and order in a portion of the globe which hitherto has seldom been blessed by these celestial visitants.

I hold that we have laid the foundation of a state of affairs which may open a new continent to the civilization of Europe, and that the welfare of the world and the wealth of the world may be increased by availing ourselves of that tranquillity and order which the more intimate connection of England with that country will now produce.

But I am sorry to say that though we taxed our brains and our thought to establish a policy which might be beneficial to the country, we have not satisfied those who are our critics.

I was astonished to learn that the Convention of the fourth of June has been described as 'an insane convention'. It is a strong epithet. I do not myself pretend to be as competent a judge of insanity as my right honourable opponent [Gladstone]. I would put this issue to an English jury – Which do you believe the most likely to enter into an insane convention – a body of English gentlemen honoured by the favour of their Sovereign and the confidence of their fellow-subjects, managing your affairs for five years, I hope with prudence, and not altogether without success, or a sophisticated rhetorician, inebriated with the exuberance of his own verbosity, and gifted with an egostical imagination that can at all times command an interminable and inconsistent series of arguments to malign an opponent and to glorify himself?

My Lords and Gentlemen, I leave the decision upon that Convention to the Parliament and people of England. I believe that in that policy are deeply laid the seeds of future welfare not merely to England, but to Europe and Asia; and confident that the policy we have recommended is one that will be supported by the country, I and those that act with me can endure these attacks.

John Bright

1811 – 1889

A leader of Victorian radicals, Bright inveighed against the establishment, both civic and ecclesiastical. He and Cobden were the twin forces behind the Anti-Corn Law League to abolish import duties on corn, but whereas Cobden persuaded the understanding, Bright excited the emotions. According to some, his task was easy. Trollope wrote: 'I think that when once he had learnt the art of arranging his words as he stood on his legs, and had so mastered his voice as to have obtained the ear of the House, the work of his life was not difficult. Having nothing to construct, he could always deal with generalities. Being free from responsibility, he was not called upon either to study details or to master even great facts. It was his business to inveigh against evils, and perhaps there is no easier business.'

At the height of the agitation against the Corn Laws, on 19 December 1845, and when millions in Ireland were threatened with famine, Bright spoke at the Covent Garden Theatre:

They sometimes think we are hard upon the aristocracy. They think that the vast populations of Lancashire and Yorkshire are democratic and turbulent. But there are no elements there, except that of great numbers, which are to be compared in their dangerous character with the elements of disaffection and insubordination which exist round about the halls and castles of this proud and arrogant aristocracy. You have seen in the papers, within the last fortnight, that the foul and frightful crime of incendiarism has again appeared. It always shows itself when we have had for some short time a high price of bread. The Corn Law is as great a robbery of the man who follows the plough as it is of him who minds the loom, with this difference, that the man who follows the plough is, of the two, nearest the earth, and it takes less power to press him into it. Mr Benett, one of the Members from Wiltshire, at an agricultural meeting held not long since, made a very long speech, in which he said some remarkable things – the most remarkable being, that if he had again to come into the world, and had the option of choosing the particular rank or class in society to which he would belong, after reviewing, I believe, a period of about seventy years, he confessed that he would choose to be an agricultural labourer. Now, this sentiment is certainly of a very novel character; and it is one worth examining, coming, as it did, from a man who had at one time, I am told, a property of eight or ten thousand a year in land.

Now, what is the condition of this agricultural labourer, for whom they tell us Protection is necessary? He lives in a parish whose owner, it may be, has deeply mortgaged it. The estate is let to farmers without capital, whose land grows almost as much rushes as wheat. The bad cultivation of the land provides scarcely any employment for the labourers, who become more and more numerous in the parish; the competition which there is amongst these labourers for the little employment to be had, bringing down the wages to the very lowest point at which their lives can be kept in them. They are heart-broken, spirit-broken, despairing men. They have been accustomed to this from their youth, and they see nothing in the future which affords a single ray of hope. We have attended meetings in those districts, and have been received with the utmost enthusiasm by these round-frocked labourers. They would have carried us from the carriage which we had travelled in, to the hustings; and if a silly squire or a foolish farmer attempted any disturbance or improper interference, these round-frocked men were all around us in an instant, ready to defend us; and I have seen them hustle many a powerful man from the field in which the meeting was being held.

Leabharlann Átha Cliath

If there be one view of this question which stimulates me to harder work in this cause than another, it is the fearful sufferings which I know to exist amongst the rural labourers in almost every part of this kingdom. How can they be men under the circumstances in which they live? During the period of their growing up to manhood, they are employed at odd jobs about the farm or the farm-yard, for wages which are merely those of little children in Lancashire. Every man who marries is considered an enemy to the parish; every child who is born into the world, instead of being a subject of rejoicing to its parents and to the community, is considered as an intruder come to compete for the little work and the small quantity of food which is left to the population. And then comes toil, year after year, long years of labour, with little remuneration; but perhaps at sixty or seventy, a gift of 20s and a coat, or of £2, from the Agricultural Society, because they have brought up a large family, and have not committed that worst of all sins, taken money from the parochial rates. One of their own poets has well expressed their condition:

> *A blessed prospect –*
> *To slave while there is strength – in age the workhouse,*
> *A parish shell at last, and the little bell*
> *Toll'd hastily for a pauper's funeral!*

But the crowning offence of the system of legislation under which we have been living is that a law has been enacted, in which it is altogether unavoidable that these industrious and deserving men should be brought down to so helpless and despairing a condition. By withdrawing the stimulus of competition, the law prevents the good cultivation of the land of our country, and therefore diminishes the supply of food which we might derive from it. It prevents, at the same time, the importation of foreign food from abroad, and it also prevents the growth of supplies abroad, so that when we are forced to go there for them they are not to be found. The law is, in fact, a law of the most ingeniously malignant character. It is fenced about in every possible way. The most demoniacal ingenuity could not have invented a scheme more calculated to bring millions of the working classes of this country to a state of pauperism, suffering, discontent, and insubordination than the Corn Law which we are now opposing.

80

And then a fat and sleek dean, a dignitary of the church and a great philosopher, recommends for the consumption of the people – he did not read a paper about the supplies that were to be had in the great valley of the Mississippi, but he said that there were Swede turnips and mangel-wurzel – and the Hereditary Earl Marshal of England, as if to out-Herod Herod himself, recommends hot water and a pinch of curry-powder. I was rejoiced, not for the sake of the Duke of Norfolk, for I pitied him, but still I was in my heart rejoiced when I saw the speech which he had made in Sussex. The people of England have not, even under thirty years of Corn Law influence, been sunk so low as to submit tamely to this insult and wrong. It is enough that a law should have been passed to make your toil valueless, to make your skill and labour unavailing to procure for you a fair supply of the common necessaries of life – but when to this grievous iniquity they add the insult of telling you to go, like beasts that perish, to mangel-wurzel, or to something which even the beasts themselves cannot eat, then I believe the people of England will rise, and with one voice proclaim the downfall of this odious system.

Later, Bright used his gifts as an orator to express immensely *unpopular* opinions when he opposed the Crimean War on the grounds that it was unnecessary and evil. His speech of 7 June 1855 in the House of Commons had a huge impact:

There is one subject upon which I should like to put a question to the noble Lord at the head of the Government. I shall not say one word here about the state of the army in the Crimea, or one word about its numbers or its condition. Every Member of this House every inhabitant of this country, has been sufficiently harrowed with details regarding it. To my solemn belief, thousands – nay, scores of thousands of persons – have retired to rest night after night whose slumbers have been disturbed or whose dreams have been based upon the sufferings and agonies of our soldiers in the Crimea. I should like to ask the noble Lord at the head of the Government – although I am not sure if he will feel that he can or ought to answer the question – whether the noble Lord the Member for London has power, after discussions have commenced, and as soon as there shall be established good grounds for believing that the negotiations for peace will prove successful, to enter into any armistice? ['No! No!']

I know not, Sir, who it is that says, 'No, no,' but I should like to see any man get up and say that the destruction of 200,000 human lives lost on all sides during the course of this unhappy conflict is not a sufficient sacrifice. You are not pretending to conquer territory – you are not pretending to hold fortified or unfortified towns; you have offered terms of peace which, as I understand them, I do not say are not moderate; and breathes there a man in this House or in this country whose appetite for blood is so insatiable that, even when terms of peace have been offered and accepted, he pines for that assault in which of Russian, Turk, French and English, as sure as one man dies, 20,000 corpses will strew the streets of Sebastopol? I say I should like to ask the noble Lord – and I am sure that he will feel, and that this House will feel, that I am speaking in no unfriendly manner towards the Government of which he is at the head – I should like to know, and I venture to hope that it is so, if the noble Lord the Member for London has power, at the earliest stage of these proceedings at Vienna, at which it can properly be done – and I should think that it might properly be done at a very early stage – to adopt a course by which all further waste of human life may be put an end to, and further animosity between three great nations be, as far as possible, prevented?

I appeal to the noble Lord at the head of the Government and to this House; I am not now complaining of the war – I am not now complaining of the terms of peace, nor, indeed, of anything that has been done – but I wish to suggest to this House what, I believe, thousands and tens of thousands of the most educated and of the most Christian portion of the people of this country are feeling upon this subject, although, indeed, in the midst of a certain clamour in the country, they do not give public expression to their feelings. Your country is not in an advantageous state at this moment; from one end of the kingdom to the other there is a general collapse of industry. Those Members of this House not intimately acquainted with the trade and commerce of the country do not fully comprehend our position as to the diminution of employment and the lessening of wages. An increase in the cost of living is finding its way to the homes and hearts of a vast number of the labouring population.

At the same time there is growing up – and, notwithstanding what some Hon. Members of this House may think of me, no man regrets it more than I do – a bitter and angry feeling against that class which has for a long period conducted the public affairs of this country. I like political changes when such changes are made as the result, not of passion, but of deliberation and reason. Changes so made are safe, but changes made under the influence of violent exaggeration or of the violent passions of public meetings, are not changes usually approved by this House or advantageous to the country. I cannot but notice, in speaking to gentlemen who sit on either side of this House, or in speaking to any one I meet between this House and any of those localities we frequent when this House is up – I cannot, I say, but notice that an uneasy feeling exists as to the news which may arrive by the very next mail from the East. I do not suppose that your troops are to be beaten in actual conflict with the foe, or that they will be driven into the sea; but I am certain that many homes in England in which there now exists a fond hope that the distant one may return – many such homes may be rendered desolate when the next mail shall arrive. The Angel of Death has been abroad throughout the land; you may almost hear the beatings of his wings. There is no one, as when the first-born were slain of old, to sprinkle with blood the lintel and the two sideposts of our doors, that he may spare and pass on; he takes his victims from the castle of the noble, the mansion of the wealthy, and the cottage of the poor and the lowly, and it is on behalf of all these classes that I make this solemn appeal.

———————

Henry John Temple, Third Viscount Palmerston

1784 – 1865

One of the most successful of British politicians during the first half of the nineteenth century, Palmerston was Foreign Secretary from 1830 to 1841, and from 1846 to 1851. During this period he became the most popular statesman in the country with his policy of protecting and strengthening British interests throughout the world, if necessary by brinkmanship. In 1855 at the age of seventy, he finally became Prime Minister and remained in office, with a break of only sixteen months, until his death in 1865.

Parliamentary eloquence was not Palmerston's strongest point and he often left it to Parliamentary shorthand writers to complete his half-sentences. A notable exception was the Don Pacifico speech on 25 June 1850. Don Pacifico was a Jew, living in Athens, but born in Gibraltar (and therefore a British citizen) whose house had been plundered by an Athenian mob. Palmerston eagerly took up his excessive claim for damages, and, when the Greeks refused to settle, dispatched a British squadron to seize sufficient Greek shipping to pay the claim. Queen Victoria was indignant and even Palmerston's colleagues were critical. A vote of censure was moved against him and Palmerston justified himself in a five-hour speech. From the individual case of Don Pacifico he proceeded to a fundamental justification of his entire policy which he felt had always served the honour and dignity of England. Unlike the rest of his speech, he had learned the closing passage by heart. He said that he could not blame the Opposition for trying to defeat the Government and gain power for themselves, for:

The government of a great country like this is undoubtedly an object of fair and legitimate ambition to men of all shades of opinion ... For while we have seen ... the political earthquake rocking Europe from side to side; while we have seen thrones shaken, shattered, levelled, institutions overthrown and destroyed; while in almost every country of Europe the conflict of civil war has deluged the land with blood, from the Adriatic to the Black Sea, from the Baltic to the Mediterranean; this country has presented a spectacle honourable to the people of England, and worthy of the admiration of mankind. We have shown that liberty is compatible with order; that individual freedom is reconcilable with obedience to the law. We have shown the example of a nation in which every class of society accepts with cheerfulness the lot which Providence has assigned to it; while at the same time every individual of each class is constantly striving to raise himself in the social scale – not by injustice and wrong, not by violence and illegality – but by persevering good conduct, and by the steady and energetic exertion of the moral and intellectual faculties with which his Creator has endowed him. To govern such a people as this, is indeed an object worthy of the ambition of the noblest man who lives in the land.

However, he did not think that the Government had done anything to forfeit the confidence of the country; and he therefore asked the House, to decide

whether, as the Roman, in days of old, held himself free from indignity when he could say *Civis Romanus sum*; so also a British subject, in whatever land he may be, shall feel confident that the watchful eye and the strong arm of England will protect him against injustice and wrong.

Henry Clay

1777 – 1852

Elected to the U.S. Senate when still under thirty, Clay was subsequently sent to the House of Representatives where he was immediately elected Speaker at the age of thirty-five, in 1811. In 1820, 1833 and 1850 he charmed through reluctant Congresses the three great compromises that preserved the Union until 1861.

An emotional and flamboyant speaker whose voice was once described as 'deliciously winning', Clay essentially appealed to the galleries. In 1818 he supported resolutions of censure against General Jackson in a three-day oration in the House of Representatives. The Senate adjourned to listen to him, and gentlemen refreshed ladies in the gallery by handing oranges up to them attached by handkerchiefs to long poles.

On the slave issue, Clay was an eloquent advocate of compromise. In February 1839 he said in presenting a petition from the inhabitants of Washington against the abolition of slavery in the District of Columbia:

I am no friend of slavery. The Searcher of all hearts knows that every pulsation of mine beats high and strong in the cause of civil liberty. Wherever it is safe and practicable, I desire to see every portion of the human family in the enjoyment of it. But I prefer the liberty of my own country to that of any other people, and the liberty of my own race to that of any other race. The liberty of the descendants of Africa in the United States is incompatible with the liberty and safety of the European descendants. Their slavery forms an exception – an exception resulting from a stern and inexorable necessity – to the general liberty in the United States. We did not originate, nor are we responsible for, this necessity. Their liberty, if it were possible, could only be established by violating the incontestable powers of the states and subverting the Union; and beneath the ruins of the Union would be buried, sooner or later, the liberty of both races.

He backed his 1850 Compromise with these words:

I believe from the bottom of my soul that this measure [the Compromise] is the reunion of the Union. And now let us discard all personal desires, all love of place, all hungering after the gilded crumbs which fall from the table of power. Let us forget popular fears, from whatever quarter they may spring. Let us go to the fountain of unadulterated patriotism, and, performing a solemn lustration, return divested of all selfish, sinister and sordid impunities, and think alone of our God, our country, our conscience, and our glorious Union.

Frederick Douglass

1817 – 1895

An ex-slave who escaped and became a leading editor, politician and abolitionist, Douglas was recognized as the most influential nineteenth-century American Negro.

On 4 July 1852 he ended a speech on 'The Meaning of the Fourth of July for the Negro' with the words:

At a time like this, scorching irony, not convincing argument, is needed. Oh! had I the ability, and could I reach the nation's ear, I would today pour out a fiery stream of biting ridicule, blasting reproach, withering sarcasm, and stern rebuke. For it is not light that is needed, but fire; it is not the gentle shower, but thunder. We need the storm, the whirlwind, and the earthquake. The feeling of the nation must be quickened; the conscience of the nation must be roused; the propriety of the nation must be startled; the hypocrisy of the nation must be exposed; and its crimes against God and man must be denounced.

What to the American slave is your Fourth of July? I answer, a day that reveals to him more than all other days of the year the gross injustice and cruelty to which he is the constant victim. To him your celebration is a sham; your boasted liberty an unholy license; your national greatness, swelling vanity; your sounds of rejoicing are empty and heartless; your denunciation of tyrants, brass-fronted impudence; your shouts of liberty and equality, hollow mockery; your prayers and hymns, your sermons and thanksgivings, with all your religious parade and solemnity, are to him mere bombast, fraud, deception, impiety, and hypocrisy – a thin veil to cover up crimes which would disgrace a nation of savages. There is not a nation of the earth guilty of practices more shocking and bloody than are the people of these United States at this very hour.

Go where you may, search where you will, roam through all the monarchies and despotisms of the Old World, travel through South America, search out every abuse and when you have found the last, lay your facts by the side of the everyday practises of this nation, and you will say with me that, for revolting barbarity and shameless hypocrisy, America reigns without a rival.

Abraham Lincoln

1809 – 1865

Throughout his career, first as a lawyer, then as Congressman for Illinois, and finally as President (1860–65), Lincoln was an impressive speaker.

His speeches in court as a young man revealed his natural gifts as an orator. Acting for the widow of a soldier of the Revolution whose pension had been mishandled by a pension agent, he proclaimed:

Time rolls by, the heroes of '76 have passed away. The soldier has gone to rest and now, crippled, blinded and broken, his widow comes to you and to me, gentlemen of the jury, to right her wrongs. She was not always thus. She was once a beautiful young woman. Her step was elastic; her face as fair and her voice as sweet as any that rang in the mountains of old Virginia. But now she is poor and defenceless. Out here on the prairies of Illinois, many hundreds of miles away from the scenes of her childhood, she appeals to us who enjoy the privileges achieved for us by the patriots of the Revolution for our sympathetic aid and manly protection. All I ask is, shall we befriend her?

In 1858 Lincoln stood against Stephen Douglas for the Senate. Douglas admitted: 'I shall have my hands full. He is the strong man of his Party, full of wit, facts, dates and the best stump-speaker in the West, with his droll ways and dry jokes.'

Lincoln's two Inaugural Addresses both contained passionate pleas for the unity of the United States.

The first, on 4 March 1861, ended with the words:

I am loath to close. We are not enemies but friends. We must not be enemies. Though passion may have strained, it must not break our bonds of affection. The mystic chords of memory, stretching from every battlefield and patriot grave, to every living heart and hearth stone all over this broad land, will yet swell the chorus of the Union when again touched, as surely they will be, by the better angels of our nature.

And the second, on 4 March 1865, included the following memorable passage:

Neither party expected for the war, the magnitude, or the duration, which it has already attained. Neither anticipated that the *cause* of the conflict might cease with, or even before, the conflict itself should cease. Each looked for an easier triumph, and a result less fundamental and astounding. Both read the same Bible, and pray to the same God; and each invokes His aid against the other . . . The prayers of both could not be answered; that of neither has been answered fully . . .

Lincoln ended with the words:

With malice toward none; with charity for all; with firmness in the right, as God gives us to see the right, let us strive on to finish the work we are in; to bind up the nation's wounds; to care for him who shall have borne the battle, and for his widow and his orphan – to do all which may achieve and cherish a just and lasting peace, among ourselves and with all nations.

Perhaps the most famous of all his speeches was the Gettysburg Address, given at the ceremony of dedication of the National Cemetery at Gettysburg, 19 November 1863:

Fourscore and seven years ago our fathers brought forth upon this continent a new nation, conceived in liberty, and dedicated to the proposition that all men are created equal. Now we are engaged in a great civil war, testing whether that nation, or any nation so conceived and so dedicated, can long endure. We are met on a great battlefield of that war. We have come to dedicate a portion of that field as a final resting-place of those who here gave their lives that that nation might live. It is altogether fitting and proper that we should do this. But in a larger sense we cannot dedicate, we cannot consecrate, we cannot hallow this ground. The brave men, living and dead, who struggled here, have consecrated it far above our power to add or detract. The world will little note, nor long remember, what we say here, but it can never forget what they did here. It is for us, the living, rather to be dedicated here to the unfinished work they have thus far so nobly advanced. It is rather for us to be here dedicated to the great task remaining before us, that from these honoured dead we take increased devotion to that cause for which they here gave the last full measure of devotion; that we here highly resolve that the dead shall not have died in vain, that this nation under God, shall have a new birth of freedom; and that government of the people, by the people, and for the people, shall not perish from the earth.

At the time, Lincoln observed: 'That speech fell on the audience like a wet blanket. I am distressed about it. I ought to have prepared it with more care.'

The view of *The Times* correspondent was even more damning: 'The ceremony was rendered ludicrous by some of the sallies of that poor President Lincoln who seems determined to play, in this great American union, the part of the famous Governor of Barataria. Anything more dull and commonplace it wouldn't be easy to imagine.'

Wendell Phillips

1811 – 1884

A lawyer, reformer and orator who spoke passionately and often against slavery in the years leading up to the Civil War, Phillips later turned to a succession of other causes such as prohibition and fair treatment for Indians.

On 27 January 1853, he addressed the Massachusetts Antislavery Society on 'The Philosophy of the Abolition Movement'.

Every thoughtful and unprejudiced mind must see that such an evil as slavery will yield only to the most radical treatment. If you consider the work we have to do, you will not think us needlessly aggressive, or that we dig down unnecessarily deep in laying the foundations of our enterprise. A money power of two thousand millions of dollars, as the price of slaves now range, held by a small body of able and desperate men; that body raised into a political aristocracy by special constitutional provisions; cotton, the product of slave labour, forming the basis of our whole foreign commerce, and the commercial class thus subsidized; the press bought up, the pulpit reduced to vassalage, the heart of the common people chilled by a bitter prejudice against the black race; our leading men bribed, by ambition, either to silence or open hostility; – in such a land, on what shall an Abolitionist rely? On a few cold prayers, mere lip-service, and never from the heart? On a church resolution, hidden often in its records, and meant only as a decent cover for servility in daily practice? On political parties, with their superficial influence at best, and seeking ordinarily only to use existing prejudices to the best advantage? Slavery has deeper root here than any aristocratic institution has in Europe; and politics is but the common pulse-beat, of which revolution is the fever-spasm. Yet we have seen European aristocracy survive storms which seemed to reach down to the primal strata of European life. Shall we, then, trust to mere politics, where even revolution has failed? How shall the stream rise above its fountain? Where shall our church organizations or parties get strength to attack their great parent and moulder, the Slave Power? Shall the thing formed say to him that formed it, Why hast thou made me thus? The old jest of one who tried to lift himself in his own basket, is but a tame picture of the man who imagines that, by working solely through existing sects and parties, he can destroy slavery. Mechanics say nothing but an earthquake, strong enough to move all Egypt, can bring down the pyramids.

Experience has confirmed these views. The Abolitionists who have acted on them have a 'short method' with all unbelievers. They have but to point to their own success, in contrast with every other man's failure. To waken the nation to its real state, and chain it to the consideration of this one duty, is half the work. So much we have done. Slavery has been made the question of this generation. To startle the South to madness, so that every step she takes, in her blindness, is one step more toward ruin, is much. This we have done. Witness Texas and the Fugitive Slave Law. To have elaborated for the nation the only plan of redemption, pointed out the only exodus from this 'sea of troubles', is much. This we claim to have done in our motto of IMMEDIATE, UNCONDITIONAL EMANCIPATION ON THE SOIL. The closer any statesmanlike mind looks into the question, the more favour our plan finds with it. The Christian asks fairly of the infidel, 'If this religion be not from God, how do you explain its triumph, and the history of the first three centuries?' Our question is similar. If our agitation has not been wisely planned and conducted, explain for us the history of the last twenty years! Experience is a safe light to walk by, and he is not a rash man who expects success in future from the same means which have secured it in times past.

John Brown
1800 – 1859

A militant opponent of slavery in the years leading up to the Civil War, John Brown was sentenced to death on 2 November 1859 after being found guilty of seizing the arsenal at Harpers Ferry, West Virginia. After being sentenced to death, he made this speech to the Court:

I have, may it please the Court, a few words to say.

In the first place, I deny everything but what I have all along admitted: of a design on my part to free slaves. I intended certainly to have made a clean thing of that matter, as I did last winter, when I went into Missouri and there took slaves without the snapping of a gun on either side, moving them through the country, and finally leaving them in Canada. I designed to have done the same thing again on a larger scale. That was all I intended. I never did intend murder, or treason, or the destruction of property, or to excite or incite slaves to rebellion, or to make insurrection.

I have another objection, and that is that it is unjust that I should suffer such a penalty. Had I interfered in the manner which I admit, and which I admit has been fairly proved – for I admire the truthfulness and candour of the greater portion of the witnesses who have testified in this case – had I so intefered in behalf of the rich, the powerful, the intelligent, the so-called great, or in behalf of any of their friends, either father, mother, brother, sister, wife or children, or any of that class, and suffered and sacrificed what I have in this interference, it would have been all right. Every man in this Court would have deemed it an act worthy of reward rather than punishment.

This Court acknowledges, too, as I suppose, the validity of the law of God. I see a book kissed, which I suppose to be the Bible, or at least the New Testament, which teaches me that all things whatsoever I would that men should do to me, I should do even so to them. It teaches me, further, to remember them that are in bonds as bound with them. I endeavoured to act up to that instruction. I say I am yet too young to understand that God is any respecter of persons. I believe that to have interfered as I have done, as I have always freely admitted I have done, in behalf of His despised poor, I did no wrong, but right. Now, if it is deemed necessary that I should forfeit my life for the furtherance of the ends of justice, and mingle my blood further with the blood of my children and with the blood of millions in this slave country whose rights are disregarded by wicked, cruel, and unjust enactments, I say, let it be done.

Let me say one word further. I feel entirely satisfied with the treatment I have received on my trial. Considering all the circumstances, it has been more generous than I expected. But I feel no consciousness of guilt. I have stated from the first what was my intention, and what was not. I never had any design against the liberty of any person, nor any disposition to commit treason or incite slaves to rebel or make any general insurrection. I never encouraged any man to do so, but always discouraged any idea of that kind.

Let me say, also, in regard to the statements made by some of those who were connected with me, I hear it has been stated by some of them that I have induced them to join me. But the contrary is true. I do not say this to injure them, but as regretting their weakness. Not one but joined me of his own accord, and the greater part at their own expense. A number of them I never saw, and never had a word of conversation with, till the day they came to me, and that was for the purpose I have stated.

Now, I have done.

William Lloyd Garrison

1805 – 1879

President of the American Anti-Slavery Society and an eloquent abolitionist speaker, Garrison said in a speech made in Boston on 2 December 1859 after hearing of the execution of John Brown:

By the dissolution of the Union we shall give the finishing blow to the slave system; and then God will make it possible for us to form a true, vital, enduring, all-embracing Union, from the Atlantic to the Pacific – one God to be worshipped, one Saviour to be revered, one policy to be carried out – freedom everywhere to all the people, without regard to complexion or race – and the blessing of God resting upon us all! I want to see that glorious day! Now the South is full of tribulation and terror and despair, going down to irretrievable bankruptcy, and fearing each bush an officer! Would to God it might all pass away like a hideous dream! and how easily it might be! What is it that God requires of the South to remove every root of bitterness, to allay every fear, to fill her borders with prosperity? But one simple act of justice, without violence and convulsion, without danger and hazard. It is this: 'Undo the heavy burdens, break every yoke, and let the oppressed go free!' Then shall thy light break forth as the morning, and thy darkness shall be as the noonday. Then shall thou call and the Lord shall answer; thou shalt cry, and he shall say: 'Here I am.' 'And they that shall be of thee shall build the old waste places; thou shalt raise up the foundations of many generations; and thou shalt be called the repairer of the breach, the restorer of paths to dwell in.'

How simple and how glorious! It is the complete solution of all the difficulties in the case. Oh, that the South may be wise before it is too late, and give heed to the word of the Lord! But, whether she will hear or forbear, let us renew our pledges to the cause of bleeding humanity, and spare no effort to make this truly the land of the free and the refuge of the oppressed!

> *Onward, then, ye fearless band,*
> *Heart to heart, and hand to hand;*
> *Yours shall be the Christian's stand,*
> *Or the martyr's grave.*

Jefferson Davis

1808 – 1889

President of the Confederate States of America during the Civil War, Davis announced Mississippi's decision to secede from the Union in a speech in the Senate on 21 January 1861. He ended with the words:

I am sure I feel no hostility to you, Senators from the North. I am sure there is not one of you, whatever sharp discussion there may have been between us, to whom I cannot now say, in the presence of my God, I wish you well; and such, I am sure, is the feeling of the people whom I represent toward those whom you represent. I therefore feel that I but express their desire when I say I hope, and they hope, for peaceful relations with you, though we must part. They may be mutually beneficial to us in the future, as they have been in the past, if you so will it. The reverse may bring disaster on every portion of the country; and if you will have it thus, we will invoke the God of our fathers, who delivered them from the power of the lion, to protect us from the ravages of the bear; and thus, putting our trust in God, and in our own firm hearts and strong arms, we will vindicate the right as best we may.

In the course of my service here, associated at different times with a great variety of senators, I see now around me some with whom I have served long; there have been points of collision; but whatever of offence there has been to me, I leave here; I carry with me no hostile remembrance. Whatever offence I have given which has not been redressed, or for which satisfaction has not been demanded, I have, senators, in this hour of our parting, to offer you my apology for any pain which, in heat of discussion, I have inflicted. I go hence unencumbered of the remembrance of any injury received, and having discharged the duty of making the only reparation in my power for any injury offered.

Mr President and Senators, having made the announcement which the occasion seemed to me to require, it only remains for me to bid you a final adieu.

Stephen Arnold Douglas

1813 – 1861

Stephen Douglas was a self-educated lawyer whose career ran parallel to that of Abraham Lincoln from the 1830s when they both sat in the Illinois State Assembly until 1860 when Lincoln defeated Douglas in the Presidential election.

Only five feet tall but with a tremendous voice, his speeches were said by Harriet Beecher Stowe, to resemble 'a bomb which hits nothing in particular, but bursts and sends red hot nails in every direction'. According to another correspondent, in 1858: 'He has no flights of fancy, no splendid passages, no prophetic appeals, no playful turns; he deals only in argument, and addresses only the intellect.'

After his defeat in the Presidential campaign, he returned to Illinois, and, in perhaps the most moving speech of his career, he addressed the Illinois legislature (25 April 1861) on the threat of Civil War. Men were said to have wept and cheered by turns, and he ended with the words:

I have struggled almost against hope to avert the calamities of war, and to effect a reunion and reconciliation with our brethren of the South. I yet hope it may be done, but I am not able to point out to you how it may be effected . . .

I see no path of ambition open in a bloody struggle for triumph over my own countrymen. There is no path of ambition open for me in a divided country, after having so long served a united and glorious country. Hence, whatever we may do must be the result of conviction of patriotic duty – the duty that we owe to ourselves, to our posterity, and to the friends of constitutional liberty and self-government throughout the world.

My friends, I can say no more. To discuss these topics is the most painful duty of my life. It is with a sad heart – with a grief that I have never before experienced, that I have to contemplate this fearful struggle; but I believe in my conscience that it is a duty we owe ourselves, and our children, and our God, to protect this Government and that flag from every assailant, be he who he may.

Edward Everett

1794 – 1865

A prominent American politician, Edward Everett was also regarded as the outstanding orator of his day. It was he who gave the main address at the consecration of the cemetery at Gettysburg in November 1863, in which he said:

And now, friends, fellow-citizens of Gettysburg and Pennsylvania, and you from remoter States, let me again, as we part, invoke your benediction on these honoured graves. You feel, though the occasion is mournful, that it is good to be here. You feel that it was greatly auspicious for the cause of the country, that the men of the East and the men of the West, the men of nineteen sister States, stood side by side, on the perilous edges of the battle. You now feel it a new bond of union, that they shall lie side by side, till a clarion, louder than that which marshalled them to the combat, shall awake their slumbers. God bless the Union; – it is dearer to us for the blood of brave men which has been shed in its defence. The spots on which they stood and fell; these pleasant heights; the fertile plain beneath them; the thriving village whose streets so lately rang with the strange din of war; the fields beyond the ridge, where the noble Reynolds held the advancing foe at bay, and, while he gave up his own life, assured by his forethought and self-sacrifice the triumph of the two succeeding days; the little streams which wind through the hills, on whose banks in after-times the wondering ploughman will turn up, with the rude

97

weapons of savage warfare, the fearful missiles of modern artillery; Seminary Ridge, the Peach-Orchard, Cemetery, Culp, and Wolf Hill, Round Top, Little Round Top, humble names, henceforward dear and famous – no lapse of time, no distance of space, shall cause you to be forgotten. 'The whole earth,' said Pericles, as he stood over the remains of his fellow citizens who had fallen in the first year of the Peloponnesian War – 'the whole earth is the sepulchre of illustrious men.' All time, he might have added, is the millennium of their glory. Surely I would do no injustice to the other noble achievements of the war, which have reflected such honour on both arms of the service, and have entitled the armies and the navy of the United States, their officers and men, to the warmest thanks and the richest rewards which a grateful people can pay. But they, I am sure, will join us in saying, as we bid farewell to the dust of these martyr-heroes that wheresoever throughout the civilized world the accounts of this great warfare are read, and down to the latest period of recorded time in the glorious annals of our common country, there will be no brighter page than that which relates the Battle of Gettysburg.

Susan B. Anthony

1820 – 1906

An early campaigner for women's suffrage in the United States, Susan Anthony was arrested in 1862 for casting a vote in the Presidential election. She refused to pay the fine which resulted, and the following year made this militant speech:

Friends and fellow citizens – I stand before you tonight under indictment for the alleged crime of having voted at the last Presidential election, without having a lawful right to vote. It shall be my work this evening to prove to you that in thus voting, I not only committed no crime, but, instead, simply exercised my *citizens' rights*, guaranteed to me and all United States citizens by the National Constitution, beyond the power of any State to deny.

The preamble of the Federal Constitution says:

'We, the people of the United States, in order to form a more perfect union, establish justice, insure *domestic* tranquillity, provide for the common defence, promote the general welfare, and secure the blessings of liberty to ourselves and our posterity, do ordain and establish this Constitution for the United States of America.'

It was we, the people; not we, the white male citizens; nor yet we, the male citizens; but we, the whole people, who formed the Union. And we formed it, not to give the blessings of liberty, but to secure them; not to the half of ourselves and the half of our posterity, but to the whole people – women as well as men. And it is a downright mockery to talk to women of their enjoyment of the blessings of liberty while they are denied the use of the only means of securing them provided by this democratic-republican Government – the ballot.

For any State to make sex a qualification that must ever result in the disfranchisement of one entire half of the people is to pass a bill of attainder, or an *ex post facto* law, and is therefore a violation of the supreme law of the land. By it the blessings of liberty are for ever withheld from women and their female posterity. To them this Government has no just powers derived from the consent of the governed. To them this Government is not a democracy. It is not a republic. It is an odious aristocracy; a hateful oligarchy of sex; the most hateful aristocracy ever established on the face of the globe; an oligarchy of wealth, where the rich govern the poor. An oligarchy of learning, where the educated govern the ignorant, or even an oligarchy of race, where the Saxon rules the African, might be endured; but this oligarchy of sex, which makes father, brothers, husband, sons, the oligarchs over the mother and sisters, the wife and daughters of every household – which ordains all men sovereigns, all women subjects, carries dissension, discord and rebellion into every home of the nation.

Webster, Worcester and Bouvier all define a citizen to be a person in the United States, entitled to vote and hold office.

The only question left to be settled now is: Are women persons? And I hardly believe any of our opponents will have the hardihood to say they are not. Being persons, then, women are citizens; and no State has a right to make any law, or to enforce any old law, that shall abridge their privileges or immunities. Hence, every discrimination against women in the constitutions and laws of the

99

several States is today null and void, precisely as in every one against negroes.

Lord Randolph Spencer Churchill

1849 – 1894

Randolph Churchill made his name as a speaker in the House of Commons but was equally successful in speeches made around the country. His audiences loved his wild abuse of the Liberal leaders, especially Gladstone. 'Give it 'em hot, Randy!' they urged. In these attacks, Churchill was at the same time trying to win supremacy for himself as Tory leader. A good example of his stinging attacks on political opponents is a speech he made at Hull on 31 October 1881:

In the diffusion of the last gospel of plunder, we may truly say that Davitt planted, Parnell watered, but Gladstone gave the increase. The planter and the waterer are laid by the heels in prison; but the man for whose benefit all these wild scenes have been enacted, for whose triumphs whole hecatombs of victims have been immolated, the great fructifier of this crop of dragon's teeth is Prime Minister of England – and that, Gentlemen, is Mr Gladstone's notion of 'the divine light of Justice!' . . .

As long as the Queen's laws have been broken he did not mind. They were unjust laws. As long as the Queen's forces were stoned and routed by the mob he could bear it; but the moment his own [Land] Act was derived, the moment that his own land court was menaced with 'boycotting' by the Land League, then the aspect of affairs changed altogether . . .

He seats himself on thrones of green and gold in Leeds Town Hall; he runs hastily after addresses in gold boxes, proffered to him by obsequious and servile Lord Mayors. He is escorted through the streets by multitudes of well-drilled caucuses waving torches and shouting loud hosannas – and, like King Herod on his throne, he may imagine that his glory also is immortal . . . Conservatives, Peelites, Whigs – he has deserted them all in turn; but ever and always he has exhibited a consuming desire for the gratification of personal vanity, and an inextinguishable lust for momentary renown, no matter by what means or at what cost it was achieved . . .

One of Churchill's best speeches was made at Blackpool on 24 January 1884 in which he attacked both Chamberlain and Gladstone before making an outspoken attack on the doctrine of *laissez-faire*:

Your iron industry is dead; dead as mutton. Your coal industries, which depend greatly upon the iron industries, are languishing. Your silk industry is dead, assassinated by the foreigner. Your woollen industry is *in articulo mortis*, gasping, struggling. Your cotton industry is seriously sick. The shipbuilding industry, which held out longest of all, is come to a standstill. Turn your eyes where you like, survey any branch of British industry you like, you will find signs of mortal disease. The self-satisfied Radical philosophers will tell you it is nothing; they point to the great volume of British trade. Yes, the volume of British trade is still large, but it is a volume which is no longer profitable; it is working and struggling. So do the muscles and nerves of the body of a man who has been hanged twitch and work violently for a short time after the operation. But death is there all the same, life has utterly departed and suddenly comes the *rigor mortis* . . . But what has produced this state of things? Free imports? I am not sure; I should like an inquiry; but I suspect free imports of the murder of our industries much in the same way as if I found a man standing over a corpse and plunging his knife into it I should suspect that man of homicide, and I should recommend a coroner's inquest and a trial by jury . . .

Samuel Dickinson Burchard

1812 – 1891

Burchard, Presbyterian minister, was on 29 October 1884 spokesman for a body of several hundred American clergymen who called on the Republican Presidential candidate James Blaine to assure him of their support. His address contained the words:

We expect to vote for you next Tuesday. We have higher expectations, which are that you will be the President of the United States and that you will do honour to your name and to the high office you will occupy. We are Republicans and don't propose to leave our party and identify ourselves with the party whose antecedents are rum, Romanism, and rebellion.

Blaine's opponent Grover Cleveland won the election.

Charles Stewart Parnell

1846 – 1891

Charles Parnell's first political speech was a disaster. At a meeting in March 1874 the owner of an Irish newspaper proposed Parnell to be Home Rule League candidate for Dublin county, and reported of his ensuing speech: 'To our dismay he broke down utterly. He faltered, he paused, went on, got confused, and pale with intense but subdued nervous anxiety, caused everyone to feel deep sympathy for him. The audience saw it all, cheered him kindly and heartily; but many on the platform shook their heads, sagely prophesying that if ever he got to Westminster, no matter how long he stayed there, he would either be a "silent member", or be known as "single-speech Parnell!" '

A year later he became an M.P., and at the height of his influence, he controlled the forces of Irish nationalism and almost succeeded in negotiating for them Home Rule for Ireland. He retained his dislike for public speaking, but became on occasions an inspiring speaker.

In January 1885 Parnell first stated explicitly that he was aiming at the restitution of a parliament for Ireland like the one Grattan had brought about in 1782. He said on 21 January at Cork:

We cannot ask for less than the restitution of Grattan's Parliament ... We cannot under the British Constitution ask for more than the restitution of Grattan's Parliament, but no man has the right to fix the boundary to the march of a nation. No man has a right to say to his country, 'Thus far shalt thou go and no further', and we have never attempted to fix the *ne plus ultra* to the progress of Ireland's nationhood, and we never shall.

These words were later engraved on the statue of Parnell that stands in Dublin.

William Ewart Gladstone

1809 – 1898

Gladstone, with Disraeli, dominated English politics in mid-Victorian England. He was Prime Minister four times between 1868 and 1894, despite the immense dislike of Queen Victoria, who complained: 'He speaks to Me as if I was a public meeting.'

To others, however, he was a wonder. A militant Irishman, William O'Brien, wrote during Gladstone's efforts on behalf of Home Rule for Ireland: 'The shorthand note is powerless . . . to bequeath to after times any adequate notion of the untranslatable things which were after all the soul of his greatness as an orator – the massive figure set foursquare to all the world's contumely in a great cause – the immense leonine head framed in its silvery mane – the great kindled eye whose expression changed in the course of a single speech from majesty to scorn and from scorn to fun, and back again to heaven-kissing sublimity – above all the uncomparable melody of a voice which had the power of transmuting common words into a no less grand but a more tender Gregorian chant.'

On 8 June 1886 Gladstone brought the debate on the Home Rule Bill to an end with the words:

Ireland stands at your bar, expectant, hopeful, almost suppliant. Her words are the words of truth and soberness. She asks a blessed oblivion of the past, and in that oblivion our interest is deeper than even here ... So I hail the demand of Ireland for what I call a blessed oblivion of the past. She asks also a boon for the future; and that boon for the future, unless we are much mistaken, will be a boon to us in respect of honour no less than a boon to her in respect of happiness, prosperity and peace ...

Think, I beseech you, think well, think wisely, think not for a moment but for the years that are to come, before you reject this Bill.

John Bright, a determined opponent of the Bill, refused to listen to Gladstone's speech. 'Once I had heard him I could not have trusted myself,' he was reported to have said.

Earlier in his career Gladstone had been equally eloquent on other subjects. In 1876 he led a campaign against atrocities committed in the Balkans by Turks. Disraeli, by this time Lord Beaconsfield, had maintained an attitude of friendship towards Turkey, and on 7 May 1877 Gladstone thundered in the House:

There were other days when England was the hope of freedom. Wherever in the world a high aspiration was entertained, or a noble blow was struck, it was to England that the eyes of the oppressed were always turned – to this favourite, this darling home of so much privilege and so much happiness, where the people that had built a noble edifice for themselves would, it was well known, be ready to do what in them lay to secure the benefit of the same inestimable boon for others. You talk to me of the established tradition and policy in regard to Turkey. I appeal to one established tradition, older, wiser, nobler far – a tradition not which disregards British interests, but which teaches you to seek for promotion of those interests in obeying the dictates of honour and of justice ... There is now before the world a glorious prize. A portion of those as yet unhappy people are still making an effort to retrieve what they have lost so long, but have not ceased to love and desire ... They seek to be diverted from an intolerable burden of woe and shame. That burden of woe and shame – the greatest that exists on God's earth – is one that we thought united

Europe was about to remove . . . the removal of that load of woe and shame is a great and noble prize. It is a prize worth competing for. It is not yet too late to win it . . . but be assured that whether you mean to claim for yourselves even a single leaf in that immortal chaplet of renown, which will be the reward of true labour in that cause, or whether you turn your backs upon that cause and your own duty, I believe for one that the knell of Turkish tyranny in those provinces has sounded. So far as human eye can judge, it is about to be destroyed. The destruction may not come in the way or by the means we should choose; but come this boon from what hands it may, it will be a noble boon, and as a noble boon it will gladly be accepted by Christendom and by the world.

James Kier Hardie

1856 – 1915

Brought up in extreme poverty, Hardie was put to work down a mine at the age of ten, and his first political activities were to try and improve the lot of the miner. In 1892 he was elected as an independent Labour M.P. and from that date until his death he worked zealously to establish the political labour movement in England.

Often successful as a speaker in the country, he never won over the House of Commons. A Lobby correspondent reported: 'The House listens to him because of the touch of tragic earnestness in his style. But it never does more than listen; he is not persuasive.'

He might not have been persuasive, but provocative he certainly was. On 28 June 1894 he attacked a proposal that the Duke and Duchess of York (the future George V and Queen Mary) should be congratulated on the birth of a son. His protest drew its emotional force from the fact that the Government had refused Hardie's request to propose a motion of condolence for the relatives of 250 miners who had been killed in a colliery explosion in South Wales a few days earlier:

Mr Speaker, on my own behalf and those whom I represent, I am unable to join in this public address. I owe no allegiance to any hereditary ruler – and I will expect those who do to allow me the ordinary courtesies of debate. The Resolution . . . seeks to elevate to an importance which it does not deserve an event of everyday occurrence ... When we are asked as the House of Commons representing the nation to join in these congratulations, then in the interests of the dignity of the House I take leave to protest.

... From his childhood onward this boy will be surrounded by sycophants and flatterers by the score – [cries of 'Oh! Oh!'] – and will be taught to believe himself as of a superior creation ... A line will be drawn between him and the people whom he is to be called upon some day to reign over. In due course, following the precedent which has already been set, he will be sent on a tour round the world, and probably rumours of a morganatic alliance will follow 'loud cries of 'Oh! Oh!' and 'Order!' and 'Question!'] – and the end of it all will be that the country will be called upon to pay the bill ... The Government will not find an opportunity for a vote of condolence with the relatives of those who are lying stiff and stark in a Welsh valley, and, if that cannot be done, the motion before the House ought never to have been proposed either. If it be for rank and title only that time and occasion can be found in this House, then the sooner that truth is known outside the better for the House itself.

Booker Washington
1856 – 1915

Born a slave, Booker Washington rose to become a black leader respected among whites during a period of tense racism. He spoke to full houses in city after city, the only really acceptable black speaker to many sectors of society. His style was conversational, with a limitless supply of anecdotes and jokes. 'I feel like a huckleberry in a bowl of milk', he told a Harvard audience.

On 18 September 1895, his Atlanta speech at the opening of the Cotton States and International Exposition brought him into national prominence as a moderate Negro spokesman. He spoke the language of patient acceptance of suffering:

The wisest among my race understand that the agitation of

questions of social equality is the extremest folly, and that progress in the enjoyment of all the privileges that will come to us must be the result of severe and constant struggle rather than of artificial forcing. No race that has anything to contribute to the markets of the world is long, in any degree, ostracized. It is important and right that all privileges of the law be ours, but it is vastly more important that we be prepared for the exercise of those privilgees. The opportunity to earn a dollar in a factory just now is worth infinitely more than the opportunity to spend a dollar in an opera-house.

In conclusion, may I repeat that nothing in thirty years has given us more hope and encouragement, and drawn us so near to you of the white race, as this opportunity offered by the Exposition; and here bending, as it were, over the altar that represents the results of the struggles of your race and mine, both starting practically empty-handed three decades ago, I pledge that, in your effort to work out the great and intricate problem which God has laid at the doors of the South, you shall have at all times the patient, sympathetic help of my race; only let this be constantly in mind, that, while from representations in these buildings of the product of field, of forest, of mine, of factory, letters, and art, much good will come, yet far above and beyond material benefits will be that higher good, that, let us pray God, will come, in a blotting out of sectional differences and racial animosities and suspicions, in a determination to administer absolute justice, in a willing obedience among all classes to the mandates of law. This, this, coupled with our material prosperity, will bring into our beloved South a new heaven and a new earth.

According to one reporter, not even Gladstone could have pleaded a cause more powerfully than 'this angular Negro standing in a nimbus of sunshine surrounded by the men who once fought to keep his race in bondage'.

For the rest of his life, Washington usually did little more than re-employ the conciliatory terms he had used in his Atlanta speech. However, in October 1898 in his Chicago Peace Jubilee speech, he spoke with unaccustomed directness about racial tensions within the States:

Until we conquer ourselves, I make no empty statement when I say that we shall have, especially in the Southern part of our country, a cancer gnawing at the heart of the Republic, that shall one day prove as dangerous as an attack from an army without or within.

William Jennings Bryan

1860 – 1925

After a successful legal career, Bryan entered politics in 1890, and in July 1896 at the Chicago Convention won the Democratic Presidential nomination on the fifth ballot, at the remarkably young age of thirty-six. He won the nomination with his famous 'Cross of Gold' speech in which he spoke for silver against gold, or for Western farmers against the industrial East.

The silver forces, he said, came not as petitioners, but as a victorious army:

We have petitioned and our petitions have been scorned; we have entreated and our entreaties have been disregarded; we have begged, and they have mocked when our calamity came. We beg no longer; we entreat no more; we petition no more. We defy them . . .

You come to us and tell us that the great cities are in favour of the gold standard; we reply that the great cities rest upon our broad and fertile prairies. Burn down your cities and leave our farms, and your cities will spring up again as if by magic; but destroy our farms and the grass will grow in the streets of every city in the country . . . Having behind us the producing masses of the nation and the world, supported by the commercial interests, the labouring interests, and the toilers everywhere, we will answer their demand for a gold standard by saying to them: You shall not press down upon the brow of labour this crown of thorns, you shall not crucify mankind upon a cross of gold.

Albert J. Beveridge

1862 – 1927

United States Senator from Indiana, Beveridge was much in demand as a public speaker. On 15 February 1899 he made a speech to the Union League Club in Philadelphia, ending with these words:

Imperialism is not the word for our vast work. Imperialism, as used by the opposers of national greatness, means oppression, and we oppress not. Imperialism, as used by the opposers of national destiny, means monarchy, and the days of monarchy are spent. Imperialism, as used by the opposers of national progress, is a word to frighten the faint of heart, and so is powerless with the fearless American people.

The Republic never retreats. Its flag is the only flag that has never known defeat. Where that flag leads we follow, for we know that the hand that bears it onward is the unseen hand of God. We follow the flag and independence is ours. We follow the flag and nationality is ours. We follow the flag and oceans are ruled. We follow the flag, and in Occident and Orient tyranny falls and barbarism is subdued.

We followed the flag at Trenton and Valley Forge, at Buena Vista and Chapultepec, at Gettysburg and Mission Ridge, at Santiago and Manila, and everywhere and always it means larger liberty, nobler opportunity, and greater human happiness; for everywhere and always it means the blessings of the greater Republic. And so God leads, we follow the flag, and the Republic never retreats.

Hugh Richard Heathcote Gascoyne Cecil, Baron Quickswood

1869 – 1956

Conservative M.P. for Greenwich from 1895 to 1906 and for Oxford University from 1910 to 1937, Cecil was created Baron Quickswood in 1941.

According to Asquith he was 'the best speaker in the House of Commons and indeed anywhere'. His reputation was made by a speech given on 16 May 1902 during the debates on the Education Act when he spoke of those possessing a Christian conscience without accepting Christian theology:

These men, it may be said, erect in the mansions of their hearts a splendid throne-room, in which they place objects revered and beautiful. There are laid the sceptre of righteousness and the sword of justice and mercy. There is the purple robe that speaks of the unity of love and power, and there is the throne that teaches the supreme moral governance of the world. And that room is decorated by all that is most beautiful in art and literature. It is gemmed by all the jewels of imagination and knowledge. Yet, that noble chamber, with all its beauty, its glorious regalia, its solitary throne, is still an empty room.

He remained unmoved by his success. 'Speechmaking,' he stated at the time, 'makes me ill.'

His best speeches came in 1910 when he defended the House of Lords tooth and nail against Liberal attack. In one speech, on 30 March 1910, he said:

I look upon our Constitution with something much more than the reverence with which a man of good taste would look upon an ancient building. I look upon it as a temple of the twin deities of Liberty and Order which Englishmen have so long worshipped to the glory of their country. Let us then go into the temple, con over its stones, and saturate ourselves with its atmosphere, and then, continuing its traditions, let us adorn and embellish it. So we too shall partake of something of its renown, our figures will, perhaps, be found in it, and our names be graven on its stones. In this way we shall attain to a measure of its immortality and nigh on the eminence of its glory our fame will stand secure, safe from the waters of oblivion, safe from the tide of time.

Theodore Roosevelt

1858 – 1919

Theodore Roosevelt was promoted to the Presidency on McKinley's death in 1901 and was then elected in his own right in 1904. Both the man and his speeches symbolized an age which was predominantly confident and moralistic.

In his Inaugural Address of 4 March 1905, he proclaimed:

Much has been given to us, and much will rightfully be expected from us. We have duties to others and duties to ourselves; and we can shirk neither. We have become a great Nation, forced by the fact of its greatness into relations with the other nations of the earth; and we must behave as beseems a people with such responsibilities. Toward all other nations, large and small, our attitude must be one of cordial and sincere friendship. We must show not only in our words, but in our deeds that we are earnestly desirous of securing their good-will by acting toward them in a spirit of just and generous recognition of all their rights. But justice and generosity in a nation, as in an individual, count most when shown not by the weak but by the strong. While ever careful to refrain from wronging others, we must be no less insistent that we are not wronged ourselves. We wish peace; but we wish the peace of justice, the peace of righteousness. We wish it because we think it is right and not because we are afraid. No weak nation that acts manfully and justly should ever have cause to fear us, and no strong power should ever be able to single us out as a subject for insolent aggression.

On 15 June 1912, roused to anger by the methods used by his opponent, for the Republican nomination, W. H. Taft, he betrayed a more natural eloquence:

What happens to me is not of the slightest consequence; I am to be used, as in a doubtful battle any man is used, to his hurt or not, so long as he is useful and is then cast aside and left to die. I wish you to feel this. I mean it; and I shall need no sympathy when you are through with me . . . It would be far better to fail honourably for the cause we champion than it would be to win by foul methods the foul victory for which our opponents hope. But the victory shall be ours, and it shall be . . . by clean and honest fighting for the loftiest of causes. We fight in honourable fashion for the good of mankind; unheeding of our individual fates; with unflinching hearts and undimmed eyes; we stand at Armageddon, and we battle for the Lord.

Joseph Chamberlain

1836 – 1914

A Birmingham screw manufacturer, Joseph Chamberlain became mayor of Birmingham in 1873 but transferred to the national political scene in 1876 when he became a Liberal M.P. He resigned from Gladstone's Government over the Home Rule for Ireland Bill in 1886 and by 1891 had become Liberal Unionist leader. In June 1895 he joined forces with the Conservative Government and became Secretary of State for the Colonies, a post which he held until 1903. During this period he advocated tariff reform to protect England and her Empire and it is for this that he is now chiefly remembered.

His speeches could be vigorous: 'The day of small nations has long passed away. The day of Empires has come.' (Birmingham 12 May 1904); or even bathetic: 'We are not downhearted. The only trouble is, we cannot understand what is happening to our neighbours.' (Smethwick 18 January 1906).

He was at his best in a speech in Birmingham (July 1906) when he was celebrating his thirtieth year as an M.P. After ranging over his political career, he spoke of the economic situation:

Relatively, in proportion to our competitors, we are getting behind-hand, and when the tide of prosperity recedes ... and a time of depression follows it, the working classes especially will be the sufferers, and we shall find then that it will be impossible without a change, to find employment for the constantly increasing population of these islands. The remedy is at hand ... we can extend our trade in the best markets, with our best friends. We can benefit them in trading with them while they give us reciprocal advantage in the preference which they give for our manufactures.

In his peroration he returned to the theme of federation:

By a commercial union we can pave the way for that federation which I see constantly before me as a practical object of aspiration, that federation of free nations which will enable us to prolong in ages yet to come all the glorious traditions of the British race ... The union of the Empire must be preceded and accompanied by a better understanding, by a closer sympathy.

To secure that is the highest object of statesmanship now at the beginning of the twentieth century. If these were the last words that I were permitted to utter to you, I would rejoice to utter them in your presence and with your approval.

Two days later Chamberlain had a stroke, and for the rest of his life was unable to make a public speech.

Frederick Edwin Smith, First Earl of Birkenhead

1872 – 1930

'The cleverest man in the kingdom', according to Lord Beaverbrook. F. E. Smith, as a Conservative M.P., dominated the House with his flamboyant personality, and, as an advocate, took part in some of the most sensational cases of the time.

On 12 March 1906 he dazzled the House with his hour-long maiden speech in which he criticized the way the recent election had been won by the Liberals. It had been learned by heart and was marked by powerful raillery and bitter invective. He set the tone at the start with his remarks on Philip Snowden's speech which had preceded his own:

The Hon. Gentleman spoke with bitterness – almost with contempt – of persons possessing large incomes. I would entreat Hon. Members to make quite sure that they have cleared their minds of cant on this question . . . When I hear vague and general proposals put forward at the expense of large incomes without any precise explanation as to the principles upon which or the extent to which those incomes are to be appropriated or tapped for the service of those who are less fortunate I should like to make an elementary observation, that there are very few Members in this House whether in opposition or on the benches opposite or below the gangway whose principal business occupation it is not to provide themselves with as large an income as they honestly can.

In Belfast on 12 July 1912, the anniversary of the Battle of the Boyne and several months after the introduction of the Home Rule Bill, he addressed 120,000 Orangemen in the lashing rain:

For how long have you nourished the dreams of the patriotism of your youth out of that deep well which inspired the Battle of the Boyne? For more than two hundred years you have refreshed your own courage, and you have educated and inspired your children in the memories of that battle. But you cannot live for ever, however glorious they may be, on the memories of your ancestors. It is time for you – listen to me – to make history for yourselves, to hand down to those coming after you, and I know that with a deep sense of individual responsibility every man and woman will sign that Covenant on Ulster Day. I make this final prediction to you that in time to come when you and I may be gathered to our fathers, many a child in Ulster enjoying the fruits of your labours . . . will say, 'My ancestors won them for me long ago at the Battle of the Boyne, and in a more recent day by those who rallied round Carson, and signed the Solemn League and Covenant of 1912.'

In the House of Lords on 24 March 1920 Lord Birkenhead made what his son and biographer thought was the finest speech of his life in the debate on the Matrimonial Causes Bill. He argued that divorce should be justified after wilful desertion for three years:

What is the remedy open to a poor woman who, when she married, gave up the pitiful pursuit by which she made her living until her marriage and, relying on the marriage, is left penniless, and is left for the whole of her life unable to identify her husband, unable to obtain the slightest relief from the law? She is neither wife nor widow; she has a cold hearthstone, she had fatherless children for the rest of her life . . .

In the cases which have come to me within the last fortnight, if I had time to deal with them I could give your Lordships particulars which would bring tears to your eyes. What is a young woman of 22 to do who is, for the rest of her life, with no hope of alleviating the future, with a fugitive husband whom she can never identify, while the law says to her plainly, finally and brutally: 'We shall do nothing for you.' It is said, 'You have open to you judicial separation.' Choosing my words advisedly and being prepared with chapter and verse of a hundred cases even at a date when the Royal Commission reported, and in a thousand cases since, I say that I can prove that this state of judicial separation – admittedly the only alternative – is a hot-bed of vice.

We are told that such a woman as I have described is to remain chaste. I have only to observe that for two thousand years human nature has resisted, in the warmth of youth, these cold admonitions of the cloisters, that I do not believe that the Supreme Being has set a standard which two thousand years of Christian experience has shown that human nature in its exuberant prime cannot support.

And that divorce should again be allowed in the case of confinement for five years under the Lunacy Law:

One tragic case is within the knowledge of your Lordships. I mention no names, nor should I have even mentioned the case had not the noble Lord affected made it public in the courts. But there was the case of the bridegroom who discovered, I think at the church door, that his wife was mentally affected. Some twenty or thirty years ago that discovery was made. The whole happiness of his life was wrecked and irretrievably destroyed, and the promise of a noble house was extinguished for ever. One day I suspect men will wonder how we sustained for so long a system so savage in its conception and so devastating in its consequences.

Those who have spoken in opposition to the present proposal say with the best motives but with malignant results: 'We deny you any hope in this world. Though an honest man loves you, sin shall be the price of your union, and bastardy shall be the fate of your children.' I cannot and do not believe that society, as it is at present constituted, will for long acquiesce in a conclusion so merciless.

He concluded:

It may well be, if your Lordships send down this Bill, that in another place it will meet with a volume of support which will, at long last, remove this great blot from our civilization. I would most earnestly implore your Lordships to be the pioneers in this great reform, and if it should prove so to be, I believe that daily and nightly your Lordships' names will be breathed with unspeakable gratitude by thousands of the most unhappy of your fellow subjects; and I am sure of this, that for generations yet to be, you will be acclaimed for the wisdom and humanity of the decision taken tonight.

Through Birkenhead's eloquence the Bill passed its second reading in the House of Lords, but was then rejected by the House of Commons.

Winston Spencer Churchill
1874 – 1965

Throughout his long career, Churchill never liked to make an impromptu speech. His speeches were invariably well planned, and many of them were learned by heart. As Balfour pointed out in 1916: 'Anybody who knows my Right Honourable Friend is aware that when he makes one of these great speeches they are not the unpremeditated effusions of a hasty moment.'

Churchill did, however, have a natural eloquence which, in the words of Violet Bonham Carter, was 'built and fashioned in heroic lines'. Many of his speeches were memorable, as were his phrases. He referred to the typical member of the House of Lords as a 'one-sided, hereditary, un-purged, unrepresentative, irresponsible, absentee', and on 22 February 1906 declared on the subject of Chinese labour in South Africa:

A labour contract into which men enter voluntarily for a limited and for a brief period, under which they are paid wages which they consider adequate, under which they are not bought or sold and from which they can obtain relief on payment of seventeen pounds ten shillings, the cost of their passage, may not be a healthy or proper contract, but it cannot in the opinion of His Majesty's Government be classified as slavery in the extreme acceptance of the word without some risk of terminological inexactitude.

On 6 July 1908 as a member of the Liberal Government Churchill supported the Coal Mines (Eight Hours) Bill with the words:

The general march of industrial democracy is not towards in-adequate hours of work, but towards sufficient hours of leisure. That is the movement among the working people all over the country. They are not content that their lives should remain mere alternations between bed and factory. They demand time to look about them, time to see their homes by daylight, to see their children, time to think and read and cultivate their gardens – time, in short, to live. That is very strange, perhaps, but that is the request they have made and are making with increasing force and reason as years pass by.

No one is to be pitied for having to work hard, for nature has contrived a special reward for the man who works hard. It gives him an extra relish, which enables him to gather in a brief space from simple pleasures a satisfaction in search of which the social idler wanders vainly through the twenty-four hours. But this reward, so precious in itself, is snatched away from the man who has won it, if the hours of his labour be too severe to leave any time for him to enjoy what he has won.

On 11 September 1914 he stated his personal attitude towards the First World War at a 'Call to Arms' meeting at the London Opera House:

We did not enter upon this war with the hope of easy victory; we did not enter upon it in any desire to extend our territory, or to advance and increase our position in the world; or in any romantic desire to shed our blood and spend our money in Continental quarrels. We entered upon this war reluctantly after we had made every effort compatible with honour to avoid being drawn in, and we entered upon it with a full realization of the sufferings, losses, disappointments, vexations and anxieties, and of the appalling and sustained exertions which would be entailed upon us by our action. The war will be long and sombre. It will have many reverses of fortune and many hopes falsified by subsequent events, and we must derive from our cause and from the strength that is in us, and from the traditions and history of our race, and from the support and aid of our Empire all over the world the means to make our British plough go over obstacles of all kinds and continue to the end of the furrow, whatever the toil and suffering may be.

Churchill hated the success of Bolshevism and on 2 January 1920 spoke about it to an enthusiastic audience at Sunderland:

Was there ever a more awful spectacle in the whole history of the world than is unfolded by the agony of Russia? This vast country, this mighty branch of the human family, not only produced enough food for itself, but before the war, it was one of the great granaries of the world, from which food was exported to every country. It is now reduced to famine of the most terrible kind, not because there is no food – there is plenty of food – but because the theories of Lenin and Trotsky have fatally, and it may be finally, ruptured the means of intercourse between man and man, between workman and peasant, between town and country; because they have scattered the systems of scientific communication by rail and river on which the life of great cities depends; because they have raised class against class and race against race in fratricidal war; because they have given vast regions where a little while ago were smiling villages or prosperous townships back to the wolves and the bears; because they have driven man from civilization to a barbarism worse than the Stone Age, and have left him the most awful and pitiable spectacle in human experience, devoured by vermin, racked by pestilence, and deprived of hope.

And this is progress, this is liberty. This is Utopia! What a monstrous absurdity and perversion of the truth it is to represent the Communistic theory as a form of progress, when, at every step and at every stage, it is simply marching back into the dark ages . . .

In the thirties Churchill urged that Britain's defences should keep pace with those of Germany. On 2 May 1935 he condemned the record of the Government in that sphere:

When the situation was manageable it was neglected, and now that it is thoroughly out of hand, we apply too late to the remedies which then might have effected a cure. There is nothing new in the story. It is as old as the Sibylline books. It falls into that immense dismal category of the fruitlessness of experience and the confirmed unteachability of mankind. Want of foresight, unwillingness to act when action would be simple and effective, lack of clear thinking, confusion of counsel until the emergency comes, until self-preservation strikes its jarring gong – these are the features which constitute the endless repetition of history.

In 1939, as Churchill himself pointed out, 'If speech-making were all that were necessary, I'd have beaten Hitler long ago.'

Several days after he had been asked to form a government, he said in the House of Commons (13 May 1940):

To form an Administration of this scale and complexity is a serious undertaking in itself, but it must be remembered that we are in the preliminary stage of one of the greatest battles in history, that we are in action at many points in Norway and in Holland, that we have to be prepared in the Mediterranean, that the air battle is continuous and that many preparations have to be made here at home. In this crisis I hope I may be pardoned if I do not address the House at any length today. I hope that any of my friends and colleagues, or former colleagues, who are affected by the political reconstruction, will make all allowance for any lack of ceremony with which it has been necessary to act. I would say to the House, as I said to those who have joined this Government: 'I have nothing to offer but blood, toil, tears and sweat.'

We have before us an ordeal of the most grievous kind. We have before us many, many long months of struggle and of suffering. You ask, what is our policy? I will say: It is to wage war, by sea, land and air, with all our might and with all the strength that God can give us: to wage war against a monstrous tyranny, never surpassed in the dark, lamentable catalogue of human crime. That is our policy. You ask, What is our aim? I can answer in one word: Victory – victory at all costs, victory in spite of all terror, victory, however long and hard the road may be; for without victory, there is no survival. Let that be realized; no survival for the British Empire; no survival for the urge and impulse of the ages that mankind will move forward towards its goal. But I take up my task with buoyancy and hope. I feel sure that our cause will not be suffered to fail among men. At this time I feel entitled to claim the aid of all, and I say, 'Come, then, let us go forward together with our united strength.'

Throughout the difficult war years Churchill continued his fighting speeches in the House of Commons. These were then broadcast on the radio to a nationwide audience.

On 18 June 1940 he declared:

What General Weygand called the Battle of France is over. I expect that the Battle of Britain is about to begin. Upon this battle depends the survival of Christian civilization. Upon it depends our own British life, and the long continuity of our institutions and our Empire. The whole fury and might of the enemy must very soon be turned on us. Hitler knows that he will have to break us in this island or lose the war. If we can stand up to him, all Europe may be free and the life of the world may move forward into broad, sunlit uplands. But if we fail, then the whole world, including the United States, including all that we have known and cared for, will sink into the abyss of a new Dark Age made more sinister, and perhaps more protracted, by the lights of perverted science. Let us therefore brace ourselves to our duties, and so bear ourselves that, if the British Empire and its Commonwealth last for a thousand years, men will still say, This was their finest hour.

And on 20 August 1940:

The gratitude of every home in our island, in our Empire, and indeed throughout the world, except in the abodes of the guilty, goes out to the British airmen who, undaunted by odds, unwearied in their constant challenge and mortal danger, are turning the tide of the world war by their prowess and by their devotion. Never in the field of human conflict was so much owed by so many to so few. All hearts go out to the fighter pilots, whose brilliant actions we see with our own eyes day after day; but we must never forget that all the time, night after night, month after month, our bomber squadrons travel far into Germany, find their targets in the darkness by the highest navigational skill, aim their attacks, often under the heaviest fire, often with serious loss, with deliberate careful discrimination, and inflict shattering blows upon the whole of the technical and war-making structure of the Nazi power.

During the war, Churchill made broadcasts to other countries. Here is an extract from one to France, made in October 1940:

Frenchmen – re-arm your spirits before it is too late. Remember how Napoleon said before one of his battles: 'These same Prussians who are so boastful today were three to one at Jena, and six to one at Montmirail.' Never will I believe that the soul of France is dead. Never will I believe that her place amongst the greatest nations of the world has been lost for ever! All these schemes and crimes of Herr Hitler's are bringing upon him and upon all who belong to his system a retribution which many of us will live to see. The story is not yet finished, but it will not be so long. We are on his track, and so are our friends across the Atlantic Ocean, and your friends across the Atlantic Ocean. If he cannot destroy us, we will surely dstroy him and all his gang, and all their works. Therefore, have hope and faith, for all will come right.

Now what is it we British ask of you in this present hard and bitter time? What we ask at this moment in our struggle to win the victory which we will share with you, is that if you cannot help us, at least you will not hinder us. Presently, you will be able to weight the arm that strikes for you, and you ought to do so. But even now we believe that Frenchmen, wherever they may be, feel their hearts warm and a proud blood tingle in their veins when we have some success in the air or on the sea, or presently – for that will come – upon the land.

Remember we shall never stop, never weary, and never give in, and that our whole people and Empire have vowed themselves to the task of cleansing Europe from the Nazi pestilence and saving the world from the new Dark Ages. Do not imagine, as the German-controlled wireless tells you, that we English seek to take your ships and colonies. We seek to beat the life and soul out of Hitler and Hitlerism. That alone, that all the time, that to the end. We do not covet anything from any nation except their respect. Those Frenchmen who are in the French Empire, and those who are in so-called unoccupied France, may see their way from time to time to useful action. I will not go into details. Hostile ears are listening. As for those, to whom English hearts go out in full, because they see them under the sharp discipline, oppression and spying of the Hun – as to those Frenchmen in the occupied regions, to them I say, when they think of the future let them remember the words which Gambetta, that great Frenchman, uttered after 1870 about the future of France and what was to come: 'Think of it always: speak of it never.'

Good night then: sleep to gather strength for the morning. For the morning will come. Brightly will it shine on the brave and true, kindly upon all who suffer for the cause, glorious upon the tombs of heroes. Thus will shine the dawn. *Vive la France*! Long live also the forward march of the common people in all the lands towards their just and true inheritance, and towards the broader and fuller age.

In his speech to the Canadian Parliament on 30 December 1941 he declared:

When I warned them [the French Government] that Britain would fight on alone whatever they did, their Generals told their Prime Minister and his divided Cabinet: 'In three weeks England will have her neck wrung like a chicken.'
Some chicken! Some neck!

After the war, and his defeat in the 1945 General Election, Churchill drew attention to the danger of Russia.
In a speech given at Westminster College, Fulton, Missouri, on 5 March 1946, he said:

From Stettin in the Baltic to Trieste in the Adriatic, an iron curtain has descended across the Continent. Behind that line lie all the capitals of the ancient states of central and eastern Europe. Warsaw, Berlin, Prague, Vienna, Budapest, Belgrade, Bucharest and Sofia, all these famous cities and the populations around them lie in what I must call the Soviet sphere, and all are subject, in one form or another, not only to Soviet influence but to a very high, and in many cases, increasing measure of control from Moscow.
Police governments are pervading from Moscow. Athens alone, with its immortal glories, is free to decide its future at an election under British, American, and French observation.

He became, too, an active advocate of European unity, and in the same speech declared:

The safety of the world requires a new unity in Europe, from which no nation should be permanently outcast. It is from the quarrels

123

of the strong parent races in Europe that the world wars we have witnessed, or which occurred in former times, have sprung.

Edward Henry Carson, Baron Carson

1854 – 1935

Carson was perhaps the best and most persuasive advocate of his day, first at the Irish Bar and then, after 1893, in London. In 1892 he was returned to Parliament as one of the Members for Dublin University, but in 1910 his rising political career took a dramatic turn when he accepted the leadership of the Ulster Unionists in the House of Commons, thereby surrendering any hopes of high political office. He resigned as leader in 1921 and the latter part of his career was spent as a Lord of Appeal in Ordinary.

Carson spoke flamboyantly but always concisely and clearly, and was successful as an orator in the courts, in the House of Commons and before mass audiences.

In 1908 a thirteen-year-old boy, George Archer-Shee, had been expelled from the Royal Naval College at Osborne on the grounds that he had stolen a postal order at the college which he had then cashed at the local post office. In 1910, after a fierce legal battle, the boy's father brought a claim on a Petition of Right against the Crown. Carson's opening speech for the plaintiff on 26 July 1910 was masterly and included the following passage:

His [Mr. Archer-Shee's] son was branded as a thief and as a forger, a boy of thirteen years old was labelled and ticketed, and has been since labelled and ticketed for all his future life as a thief and a forger, and in such investigation as had occurred which led to that disastrous result, neither his father nor any friend was ever there to hear what was alleged or what was said against a boy of thirteen absolutely deprived of the possibility of any future career in His Majesty's Service, or indeed in any other Service.

Gentlemen, I protest against the injustice to a little boy, a child of thirteen years of age, without communication with his father or his parents, without his case ever being put, or an opportunity of its ever being put forward by those on his behalf. I protest against that boy at that early stage, a boy of that character, being branded for the rest of his life by that one act, an irretrievable act that I venture to think could never be got over. That little boy, from that day, and from the day that he was first charged, up to this moment – whether it was in the ordeal of being called in before his Commander and his Captain, or whether it was under the softer influences of the persuasion of his own parents – has never faltered in the statement that he is an innocent boy.

Now, Gentlemen, two years nearly have elapsed; we have pressed for an independent inquiry, not an official and departmental inquiry, but we have asked them to let us bring the boy into the open until in the end, after the circumstances that I shall tell you, we bring this Petition of Right, and then at the last moment that is objected to, until we get an order from the Court directing this trial to come before you. In that way we will now have the satisfaction of knowing that if this boy is to spend the rest of his life under this stigma as a thief and a forger it will not be by any enquiry of a department or any autocratic action of the State, but it will be the verdict of twelve of his own citizens after they have thoroughly sifted the evidence, and be he right or be he wrong, that, and that alone can be a satisfactory conclusion of this case. His father unhesitatingly puts him before you to try a charge of theft against him. He asks nothing but what the ordinary street Arab would have for his own child – nay, not so much, because before the ordinary child of the street could be condemned and convicted he would at least have the protection of a grand jury, presided over by a Judge, and he would have the protection of a common jury afterwards presided over by a Judge and the ultimate protection of the Court of Appeal. I say, Gentlemen, that letter was a disastrous letter, not only for the reason that it deprived the boy of the power of going on with his career, and his father of the possibility of continuing him in the career he had intended him for, but you know well that a department who had once taken up that attitude, however erroneously, never, if they could help it, would go back, because if the boy was not guilty it was a matter of such serious import to the Admiralty and to those who were concerned in it that they were bound to fight it and did fight it, and do fight it to the very end.

Now, Gentlemen, I do not trouble you in this case with the

technical defences that are entered here, I do not trouble you in this case with regard to the powers of the Crown to exercise rights of dismissal or anything of that kind, but I put this boy before you to be tried on the plain issues: are you satisfied that he is a thief and a forger, and they may make what they like of their legal point afterwards.

After four days, the Admiralty lawyers made a statement accepting the innocence of George Archer-Shee.

On 23 September 1911 over 100,000 Ulster men were brought face to face with their new leader at Craigavon. After listening to a number of Addresses expressing determination to resist the jurisdiction of a Dublin Parliament, Carson himself spoke in fighting terms:

I know full well what the Resolution you have just passed means. I know what all these Addresses mean. I know the responsibility you are putting on me today. In your presence I cheerfully accept it, grave as it is, and I now enter into a compact with you, and every one of you, and with the help of God you and I joined together – I giving you the best I can, and you giving me all your strength behind me – we will yet defeat the most nefarious conspiracy that has ever been hatched against a free people.

But I know full well that this Resolution has a wider meaning. It shows me that you realize the gravity of the situation that is before us, and it shows me that you are here to express your determination to see this fight out to a finish . . .

Mr Asquith, the Prime Minister, says that we are not to be allowed to put our case before the British electorate. Very well. By that determination he drives you in the ultimate result to rely upon your own strength, and we must follow all that out to its logical conclusion . . . That involves something more than that we do not accept Home Rule.

We must be prepared, in the event of a Home Rule Bill passing, with such measures as will carry on for ourselves the government of those districts of which we have control. We must be prepared – and time is precious in these things – the morning Home Rule passes, ourselves to become responsible for the government of the Protestant Province of Ulster.

Thomas Woodrow Wilson

1856 – 1924

An academic who resigned from his post as President of Princeton to become Governor of New Jersey in 1910, Wilson was nominated Democratic Presidential candidate in 1912. He won the Presidential election in that year, and was re-elected in 1916.

As a young man, Wilson had learnt by heart passages from the great English orators. Gladstone was a great favourite and Wilson's speeches, like Gladstone's, were characterized by strong moral fervour. He was, too, lucid in argument and passionately sincere. According to a contemporary: 'He was a scholar in action, a prophet touched by fire, with unmatched strength to persuade and move the hearts of his listeners.'

One of his 1912 campaign speeches best sets out his lofty idealism. It was given on 23 September at Scranton, Pennsylvania, and ended with the words:

The vision of America will never change. America once, when she was a little people, sat upon a hill of privilege and had a vision of the future. She saw men happy because they were free. She saw them free because they were equal. She saw them banded together because they had the spirit of brothers. She saw them safe because they did not wish to impose upon one another. And the vision is not changed. The multitude has grown, that welcome multitude that comes from all parts of the world to seek a safe place of life and of hope in America. And so America will move forward, if she moves forward at all, only with her face to that same sun of promise. Just so soon as she forgets the sun in the heavens, just so soon as she looks so intently upon the road before her and around her that she does not know where it leads, then will she forget what America was created for; her light will go out; the nations will grope again in darkness and they will say: 'Where are those who prophesied a day of freedom for us? Where are the lights that we followed? Where is the torch that the runners bore? Where are those who bade us hope? Where came in these whispers of dull despair? Has Amercia turned back? Has America forgotten her mission? Has America forgotten that her politics are part of her life, and that only as the red blood of her people flows in the veins of her polity shall she occupy that point of vantage which has made her the beacon and the leader of mankind?

By 2 April 1917, Wilson the pacifist was forced to appear before Congress asking for a declaration of war:

It is a fearful thing to lead this great peaceful people into war, into the most terrible and disastrous of all wars, civilization itself seeming to be in the balance. But the right is more precious than peace, and we shall fight for the things which we have always carried nearest our hearts – for democracy, for the right of those who submit to authority to have a voice in their own Government, for the rights and liberties of small nations, for a universal dominion of right by such a concert of free peoples as shall bring peace and safety to all nations and make the world itself at last free. To such a task we can dedicate our lives and our fortunes, everything that we are and everything that we have, with the pride of those who know that the day has come when America is privileged to spend her blood and her might for the principles that gave her birth and happiness and the peace which she has treasured. God helping her, she can do no other.

Emmeline Pankhurst

1858 – 1928

Leader of the crusade for women's suffrage, Emmeline Pankhurst was a powerful public speaker who could move her audience almost in the manner of a revivalist preacher.

At the Albert Hall in October 1912, for example, she stated that when women had got the vote they would again be what they were by nature and inclination – 'the most law-abiding half of the community'.

'But,' she cried in conclusion,

when anti-suffrage members of the Government criticize militancy in women, it is very like beasts of prey reproaching the gentler animals who turn in desperate resistance at the point of death. The only recklessness militant suffragists have shown has been with their own lives, not the lives of others . . . We leave that to the enemy . . . There is something that governments care for more than human life, and that is the security of property. So it is through property that we shall strike the enemy. We in the Suffragette Army have a great mission, the greatest mission the world has ever known – the freeing of one half of the human race and through that freedom the saving of the other half. I incite this meeting to rebellion!

In the dock at the Old Bailey in April 1913 on trial for conspiracy, she spoke out in defiance. Suffragettes, she said, believed that

the horrible evils which are ravaging our civilization will never be removed until women get the vote. They know that the very fount of life is being poisoned . . . that because of bad education and unequal moral standards even mothers and children are being destroyed by the vilest diseases . . . There is only one way to put a stop to this agitation – by doing us justice. I feel I have done my duty. I look upon myself as a prisoner of war under no moral obligation to conform to, or in any way accept, the sentence imposed upon me.

The jury found Mrs Pankhurst guilty but recommended leniency. She was sentenced to three years' penal servitude.

Herbert Henry Asquith, First Earl of Oxford and Asquith

1852 – 1928

A Home Secretary and Chancellor of the Exchequer before he was Liberal Prime Minister from 1908 to 1916, Asquith was an intellectual speaker who employed classical techniques to the full. According to Roy Jenkins, his biographer: 'He never had the emotional range of Gladstone or the electrifying effect of Randolph Churchill at his best, but he had a consistent power of pungent, almost unanswerable argument.'

In September 1914, a month after the outbreak of the First World War, Asquith spoke at Mansion House in London:

We were very confident three years ago in the rightness of our position when we welcomed the new securities for peace. We are equally confident in it today, when reluctantly, and against our will, but with clear judgment and a clean conscience, we find ourselves involved with the whole strength of this Empire in this bloody arbitrament between might and right. The issue has passed out of the domain of argument into another field. But let me ask you, and through you the world outside, what would have been our condition as a nation today, if through timidity, or through a perverted calculation of self-interest, or through a paralysis of the sense or honour and duty, we had been base enough to be false to our word, and faithless to our friends? Our eyes would have been turned at this moment with those of the whole civilized world to Belgium, a small State, which has lived for more than seventy years under a several and collective guarantee to which we, in common with Prussia and Austria, were parties. We should have seen, at the instance and by the action of two of those guaranteeing Powers, her neutrality violated, her independence strangled, her territory made use of as affording the easiest and most convenient road to a war of unprovoked aggression against France. We, the British people, should at this moment have been standing by, with folded arms and with such countenance as we could command, while this small and unprotected State, in defence of her vital liberties, made a heroic stand against overweening and over-whelming force. We should have been admiring as detached spectators the siege of Liège, the steady and manful resistance of a small army, the occupation of Brussels with all its splendid tradi-tions and memories, the gradual forcing back of the patriotic defenders of their fatherland to the ramparts of Antwerp, countless outrages suffered by them, buccaneering levies exacted from the unoffending civil population, and, finally, the greatest crime com-mitted against civilization and culture since the Thirty Years' War, the sack of Louvain, with its buildings, its pictures, its unique library, its unrivalled associations, a shameless holocaust of irrepar-able treasures, lit up by blind barbarian vengeance. What account could we, the government and the people of this country, have been able to render to the tribunal of our national conscience and sense of honour, if, in defiance of our plighted and solemn obli-gations, we had endured, and had not done our best to prevent, yes, to avenge, these intolerable wrongs? For my part, I say that sooner than be a silent witness, which means in effect a willing accomplice, to this tragic triumph of force over law, and brutality over freedom, I would see this country of ours blotted out of the pages of history.

That is only a phase, a lurid and illuminating phase, in the contest into which we have been called by the mandate of duty and of honour to bear our part. The cynical violation of the neutrality of Belgium was not the whole, but a step, a first step, in a deliberate policy of which, if not the immediate, the ultimate and not far distant aim was to crush the independence and the autonomy of the Free States of Europe. First Belgium, then Holland and Switzer-land, countries like our own, imbued and sustained with the spirit of liberty, were, one after another, to be bent to the yoke. And these ambitions were fed and fostered by a body of new doctrine, a new philosophy, preached by professors and learned men. The free and full self-development which to these small States, to ourselves, to our great and growing Dominions over the seas, to our kinsmen across the Atlantic, is the well-spring and life-breath of national existence, that free self-development is the one capital offence in the code of those who have made force their supreme divinity, and upon its altars they are prepared to sacrifice both the gathered fruits and the potential germs of the unfettered human spirit. I use this language advisedly. This is not merely a material, it is also a spiritual conflict. Upon its issue everything that contains the promise of hope, that leads to emancipation and a fuller liberty for the millions who make up the mass of mankind, will be found sooner or later to depend . . .

Is there anyone in this hall, or in this United Kingdom, or in the vast Empire of which we here stand in the capital and centre, who blames us or repents our decision? If not, as I believe there is not, we must steel ourselves to the task, and, in the spirit which animated our forefathers in their struggle against the dominion of Napoleon, we must, and we shall, persevere to the end.

I say nothing more, because I think we should bear in mind, all of us, that we are at present watching the fluctuation of fortune only in the early stages of what is going to be a protracted struggle We must learn to take long views and to cultivate above all other qualities – those of patience, endurance, and steadfastness.

Meanwhile, let us go, each one of us, to his or her appropriate part in the great common task.

Never had a people more or richer sources of encouragement and inspiration. Let us realize, first of all, that we are fighting as a United Empire, in a cause worthy of the highest traditions of our race. Let us keep in mind the patient and indomitable seamen who never relax for a moment, night or day, their stern vigil on the lonely sea. Let us keep in mind our gallant troops, who today, after a fortnight's continuous fighting under conditions which would try the mettle of the best army that ever took the field, maintain not only an undefeated but an unbroken front.

Finally, let us recall the memories of the great men and the great deeds of the past, commemorated some of them in the monuments which we see around us on these walls, not forgetting the dying message of the younger Pitt – his last public utterance, made at the table of your predecessor, my Lord Mayor, in this very hall, 'England has saved herself by her exertions and will, as I trust, save Europe by her example'. The England of those days gave a noble answer to his appeal and did not sheathe the sword until after nearly twenty years of fighting the freedom of Europe was secured. Let us go and do likewise.

David Lloyd George, First Earl Lloyd-George of Dwyfor

1863 – 1945

Elected Liberal M.P. for Carnarvon at the age of twenty-seven, he held the seat for fifty-five years until his acceptance of a peerage in 1945. When the Liberals came to power in 1905 he became President of the Board of Trade, and, three years later, Chancellor of the Exchequer. At the end of 1916, he was appointed Prime Minister of a Coalition Government which lasted until 1922. This was the last time he held office.

According to Harold Macmillan: 'He was the best parliamentary debater of his, or perhaps any, day. Churchill's speeches were powerful but prepared in his own style, where every word was written out beforehand. Impressive, as they might be, they lacked flexibility . . . Lloyd George who spoke from few notes commanded batteries as powerful as Churchill's but much more mobile.'

Lloyd George was equally successful in the House of Commons or at large public meetings, but interestingly he was unable to address a radio audience with the same spontaneity as he did live crowds.

On 19 September 1914, while he was Commissioner of Munitions, he ended a speech in London with the following words of encouragement in the face of war with Germany:

They think we cannot beat them. It will not be easy. It will be a long job; it will be a terrible war; but in the end we shall march through terror to triumph. We shall need all our qualities – every quality that Britain and its people possess – prudence in counsel, daring in action, tenacity in purpose, courage in defeat, moderation in victory; in all things faith.

The people will gain more by this struggle in all lands than they comprehend at the present moment. It is true they will be free of the greatest menace to their freedom. That is not all. There is something infinitely greater and more enduring which is emerging already out of this great conflict – a new patriotism, richer, nobler, and more exalted than the old. I see amongst all classes, high and low, shedding themselves of selfishness, a new recognition that the honour of the country does not depend merely on the maintenance of its glory in the stricken field, but also in protecting its homes from distress. It is bringing a new outlook for all classes. The great flood of luxury and sloth which had submerged the land is receding, and a new Britain is appearing. We can see for the first time the fundamental things that matter in life, and that have been obscured from our vision by the tropical growth of prosperity.

May I tell you in a simple parable what I think this war is doing for us? I know a valley in North Wales, between the mountains and the sea. It is a beautiful valley, snug, comfortable, sheltered by the mountains from all the bitter blasts. But it is very enervating, and I remember how the boys were in the habit of climbing the hill above the village to have a glimpse of the great mountains in the distance, and to be stimulated, and freshened by the breezes which came from the hilltops, and by the great spectacle of their grandeur. We have been living in a sheltered valley for generations. We have been too comfortable and too indulgent – many, perhaps, too selfish – and the stern hand of Fate has scourged us to an elevation where we can see the great everlasting things that matter for a nation – the great peaks we had forgotten, of Honour, Duty, Patriotism, and, clad in glittering white, the great pinnacle of Sacrifice pointing like a rugged finger to Heaven. We shall descend into the valleys again; but as long as the men and women of this generation last, they will carry in their hearts the image of those great mountain peaks whose foundations are not shaken, though Europe rock and sway in the convulsions of a great war.

On 14 December 1917, Lloyd George, now Prime Minister, spoke the following words of encouragement:

We are laying surely the foundation of the bridge which, when it is complete, will carry us into the new world. The river is, for the moment, in spate, and some of the scaffolding has been carried away and much of the progress we have made seems submerged and hidden, and there are men who say: 'Let us abandon the enterprise altogether. It is too costly. It is impracticable of achievement. Let us rather build a pontoon bridge of new treaties, league of nations, understanding.' It might last you some time. It would always be shaky and uncertain. It would not bear much strain. It would not carry heavy traffic, and the first flood would sweep it away. Let us get along with the pile-driving and make a real solid permanent structure.

There are people who are too apt at one moment to get unduly elated at victories, which are but incidents in the great march of events, and the same people get unwholesomely depressed by defeats which again are nothing more than incidents . . . They remind me of a clock I used to pass at one time in my life almost every day. It worried me a great deal, for whatever the time of day, it always pointed to twelve o'clock. If you trusted that clock you would have believed it was either noon or midnight. There are people of that type in this war who at one moment point to the high noon of triumph and the next to the black midnight of defeat or despair. There is no twilight. There is no morning. They can claim a certain consistency, for they are always at twelve; but you will find that their mainspring in this war is out of repair. We must go through all the hours, minute by minute, second by second, with a steady swing, and the hour of the dawn will in due time strike.

We have all been dreaming of a new world to appear when the deluge of war has subsided. Unless we achieve victory for the great cause for which we entered this war, the new world will simply be the old world with the heart out of it.

The old world, at least, believed in ideals. It believed that justice, fair play, liberty, righteousness must triumph in the end; that is, however you interpret the phrase, the old world believed in God, and it staked its existence on that belief. Millions of gallant young men volunteered to die for that divine faith. But if wrong emerged triumphant out of this conflict, the new world would feel in its soul that brute force alone counted in the government of man; and the hopelessness of the Dark Ages would once more fall on the earth like a cloud. To redeem Britain, to redeem Europe, to redeem the world from this doom must be the settled purpose of every man and woman who places duty above ease. This is the fateful hour of mankind. If we are worthy of the destiny with which it is charged, untold generations of men will thank God for the strength which He gave us to endure to the end.

Arthur James Balfour

1848 – 1930

Balfour held high office almost continuously from the late 1880s until 1929, and was Prime Minister from 1902 to 1905.

On 4 July 1917, as Foreign Secretary, he spoke at a Fourth of July celebration in London. He paid tribute to the United States, concluding with the words:

All I can say in excuse for my forefathers is that, utterly defective as the colonial policy of Great Britain in the middle of the eighteenth century undoubtedly was, it was far better than the colonial policy of any other country. Imperfectly as we conceived the kind of relations that might, or could, bind the colonies to their Mother Country, thoroughly as we misconceived them, we misconceived them less than most of our neighbours.

If I rightly read the signs of the times, a truer perspective and a more charitable perspective is now recognized and felt by all the heirs of these sad and ancient glories. Heaven knows I do not grudge the glories of Washington and his brother soldiers. I do not shed tears over the British defeat which ended in the triumphant establishment of the American Republic. I do not express any regrets on that subject. My only regrets are that the memories of it should carry with them the smallest trace of bitterness on our side. I do not know why these should be. I think it may properly carry memories of triumph on your side, but it should be a triumph seen in its true perspective, and by this true perspective seen in such a way that it does not interfere with the continuity of history in the development of free institutions and with the consciousness of common kinship and common ideals and the considerations which ought to bind us together, and which have bound us together, and which year by year, generation by generation, and century by century, are going to bind us still closer in the future.

Eugene Victor Debs

1855 – 1926

Leading orator of the Socialist party, and several times its candidate for the Presidency, Debs was a fervent opponent of American entry into the First World War. He was sentenced to prison after being convicted of the charge of obstructing the draft. In his speech before the Court on receiving sentence (September 1918) he proclaimed:

Your Honour, years ago I recognized my kinship with all living beings, and I made up my mind that I was not one bit better than the meanest of earth. I said then, I say now, that while there is a lower class, I am in it; while there is a criminal element, I am of it; while there is a soul in prison, I am not free.

If the law under which I have been convicted is a good law, then there is no reason why sentence should not be pronounced upon me. I listened to all that was said in this Court in support and justification of this law, but my mind remains unchanged. I look upon it as a despotic enactment in flagrant conflict with democratic principles and with the spirit of free institutions.

Your Honour, I have stated in this Court that I am opposed to the form of our present Government; that I am opposed to the social system in which we live; that I believed in the change of both – but by perfectly peaceable and orderly means.

I believe, your Honour, in common with all Socialists, that this nation ought to own and control its industries. I believe, as all Socialists do, that all things that are jointly needed and used ought to be jointly owned – that industry, the basis of life, instead of being the private property of the few and operated for their enrichment, ought to be the common property of all, democratically administered in the interest of all.

I have been accused, your Honour, of being an enemy of the

soldier. I hope I am laying no flattering unction to my soul when I say that I don't believe the soldier has a more sympathetic friend than I am. If I had my way there would be no soldiers. But I realize the sacrifice they are making. Your Honour, I can think of them. I can feel for them. I can sympathize with them. That is one of the reasons why I have been doing what little has been in my power to bring about a condition of affairs in this country worthy of the sacrifices they have made and that they are now making in its behalf.

Your Honour, I wish to make acknowledgement of my thanks to the counsel for the defence. They have not only defended me with exceptional legal ability, but with a personal attachment and devotion of which I am deeply sensible, and which I can never forget.

Your Honour, I ask no mercy. I plead for no immunity. I realize that finally the right must prevail. I never more clearly comprehended than now the great struggle between the powers of greed on the one hand and upon the other the rising hosts of freedom.

I can see the dawn of a better day of humanity. The people are awakening. In due course of time they will come to their own.

When the mariner, sailing over tropic seas, looks for relief from his weary watch, he turns his eyes toward the Southern Cross, burning luridly above the tempest-tossed ocean. As the midnight approaches, the Southern Cross begins to bend, and the whirling worlds change their places, and with starry finger-points the Almighty marks the passage of time upon the dial of the universe, and though no bell may beat the glad tidings, the lookout knows that the midnight is passing – that relief and rest are close at hand.

Let the people take heart and hope everywhere, for the cross is bending, the midnight is passing, and joy cometh with the morning.

Your Honour, I thank you, and I thank all of this court for their courtesy, for their kindness, which I shall remember always.

I am prepared to receive your sentence.

James Ramsay MacDonald
1866 – 1937

Ramsay MacDonald rose to become the first Labour Prime Minister from 1929 to 1931, and then leader of a National Government from 1931 to 1935.

According to Harold Macmillan: 'The more you listened to MacDonald the more fascinated you became by the cadence of his voice and the musical phrases of his oratory. But it was difficult to discern any very specific purpose, or any clear conclusions.'

A convinced pacifist, Ramsay MacDonald expressed his views with great passion before the Labour Party Conference in 1919:

Today, as I read about the Peace, as I hoped and prayed about the Peace, I thought of the almost countless graves scattered in the centre of Europe. Many of our children are lying there. It must be in the hearts of all of us to build a fair monument to those men who will never come back to bless us with their smiles. Do they not want a grand and magnificent monument built for them so that the next generations, even if they forget their names, shall never forget their sacrifice? That is what I want. I almost felt I heard the grass growing over them in a magnificent, soothing harmony, and that simple soothing peace of the growing grass seemed to grow louder and more magnificent until the riot and distractive sound of the guns were stifled and stilled by it. Can we not have that sentiment today, that feeling in our hearts? Can we not go in imagination to where our children lie, and feel that in Europe, in our hearts, that same peace shall rule, and through sorrow and through sacrifice we shall obtain that wisdom and light which will enable Europe to possess peace for ever?

Oliver Wendell Holmes

1841 – 1935

From 1882 to 1932 the 'Great Dissenter' sat on the Supreme Court of Massachusetts and then of the United States.

In 1919 the Supreme Court sentenced a garment-worker, Jacob Adernams, to twenty years imprisonment for distributing a pamphlet calling on the workers of the world to rise against the American military expedition to Siberia. (A small force of Americans had fought in the Archangel–Murmansk campaign of 1918–19 and another in an Allied expedition in Siberia that ended in 1920. These interventions had been motivated more by ill-founded military concerns than by a desire to crush Bolshevism.) Justice Holmes on this occasion produced a moving and eloquent dissent:

When men have realized that time has upset many fighting faiths, they may come to believe even more than they believe the very foundations of their own conduct that the ultimate good desired is better reached by free trade in ideas – that the best test of truth is the power of the thought to get itself accepted in the competition of the market, and that truth is the only ground upon which their wishes can be safely carried out. That at any rate is the theory of our Constitution. It is an experiment, as all life is an experiment. Every year if not every day we have to wager our salvation upon some prophecy based upon imperfect knowledge. While that experiment is part of our system I think that we should be eternally vigilant against attempts to check the expression of opinions that we loathe and believe to be fraught with death, unless they so imminently threaten immediate interference with the lawful and pressing purposes of the law that an immediate check is required to save the country.

Clarence S. Darrow

1857 – 1938

Darrow was an outstanding American lawyer and orator. Perhaps his most famous speech was his address for the defence in the Richard A. Loeb and Nathan F. Leopold case in 1924. These two youths, aged eighteen and nineteen respectively, had confessed to the kidnapping and murder of a fourteen-year-old neighbour, purely for the thrill involved in their deed. Darrow pleaded against capital punishment for the two defendants and managed to secure the lesser penalty of life imprisonment. He said:

There are causes for this terrible crime. There are causes, as I have said, for everything that happens in the world. War is a part of it; education is a part of it; birth is a part of it; money is a part of it – all these conspired to compass the destruction of these two poor boys.

Has the Court any right to consider anything but these two boys? The State says that your Honour has a right to consider the welfare of the community, as you have. If the welfare of the community would be benefited by taking these lives, well and good. I think it would work evil that no one could measure. Has your Honour a right to consider the families of these two defendants? I have been sorry, and I am sorry for the bereavement of Mr and Mrs Frank, for those broken ties that cannot be healed. All I can hope and wish is that some good may come from it all. But as compared with the families of Leopold and Loeb, the Franks are to be envied – everyone knows it.

I do not know how much salvage there is in these two boys. I hate to say it in their presence, but what is there to look forward to? I do not know but what your Honour would be merciful if you tied a rope around their necks and let them die; merciful to them, but not merciful to civilization, and not merciful to those who would be left behind. To spend the balance of their days in prison is mighty little to look forward to, if anything. Is it anything?

They may have the hope that as the years roll around they might be released. I do not know. I do not know. I will be honest with this court as I have tried to be from the beginning. I know that these boys are not fit to be at large. I believe they will not be until they pass through the next stage of life, at forty-five or fifty. Whether they will then, I cannot tell. I am sure of this; that I will not be here to help them. So far as I am concerned, it is over.

I would not tell this Court that I do not hope that some time, when life and age have changed their emotions, as they do – that they may once more return to life. I would be the last person on earth to close the door of hope to any human being that lives, and least of all to my clients. But what have they to look forward to? Nothing. And I think here of the stanza of Housman:

> Now hollow fires burn out to black,
> And lights are fluttering low;
> Square your shoulders, lift your pack
> And leave your friends and go.
> O never fear, lads, naught's to dread,
> Look not left nor right:
> In all the endless road you tread
> There's nothing but the night.

I care not, your Honour, whether the march begins at the gallows or when the gates of Joliet close upon them, there is nothing but the night, and that is little for any human being to expect.

But there are others to consider. Here are these two families, who have led honest lives, who will bear the name that they bear, and future generations must carry it on.

Here is Leopold's father – and this boy was the pride of his life. He watched him, he cared for him, he worked for him; the boy was brilliant and accomplished, he educated him, and he thought that fame and position awaited him, as it should have awaited. It is a hard thing for a father to see his life's hopes crumble into dust.

Should he be considered? Should his brothers be considered? Will it do society any good or make your life safer, or any human being's life safer, if it should be handed down from generation to generation, that this boy, their kin, died upon the scaffold?

And Loeb's, the same. Here are the faithful uncle and brother, who have watched here day by day, while Dickie's father and his mother are too ill to stand this terrific strain, and shall be waiting for a message which means more to them than it can mean to you or me. Shall these be taken into account in this general bereavement?

Have they any rights? Is there any reason, your Honour, why their proud names and all the future generations that bear them shall have this bar sinister written across them? How many boys and girls, how many unborn children will feel it? It is bad enough as it is, God knows. It is bad enough, however it is. But it's not yet death on the scaffold. It's not that. And I ask your Honour, in addition to all that I have said, to save two honorable families from a disgrace that never ends, and which could be of no avail to help any human being that lives.

Now, I must say a word more and then I will leave this with you where I should have left it long ago. None of us are unmindful of the public; courts are not, and juries are not. We placed our fate in the hands of a trained court, thinking that he would be more mindful and considerate than a jury. I cannot say how people feel. I have stood here for three months as one might stand at the ocean trying to sweep back the tide. I hope the seas are subsiding and the wind is falling, and I believe they are, but I wish to make no false pretence to this Court. The easy thing and the popular thing to do is to hang my clients. I know it. Men and women who do not think will applaud. The cruel and thoughtless will approve. It will be easy today; but in Chicago, and reaching out over the length and breadth of the land, more and more fathers and mothers, the humane, the kind and the hopeful, who are gaining an understanding and asking questions not only about these poor boys, but about their own – these will join in no acclaim at the death of my clients. These would ask that the shedding of blood be stopped, and that the normal feelings of man resume their sway. And as the days and the months and the years go on, they will ask it more and more. But, your Honour, what they shall ask may not count. I know the easy way. I know your Honour stands between the future and the past. I know the future is with me, and what I stand for here; not merely for the lives of these two unfortunate lads, but for all boys and all girls; for all the young, and as far as possible, for all of the old. I am pleading for life, understanding, charity, kindness, and the infinite mercy that considers all. I am pleading that we overcome cruelty with kindness and hatred with love. I know the future is on my side. Your Honour stands between the past and the future. You may hang these boys; you may hang them by the neck until they are dead. But in doing it you will turn your face toward the past. In doing it you are making it harder for every other boy who in ignorance and darkness must grope his way through the mazes which only childhood knows. In doing it you will make it harder for unborn children. You may save them and make it easier for every child that sometime may stand where these boys stand. You will make it easier for every human being with an aspiration and a vision and a hope and a fate. I am pleading for the future; I am pleading for a time when hatred and cruelty will not control the hearts of men. When we can learn by reason and judgment and understanding and faith that all life is worth saving, and that mercy is the highest attribute of man.

I feel that I should apologize for the length of time I have taken. This case may not be as important as I think it is, and I am sure I do not need to tell this court, or to tell my friends that I would fight as hard for the poor as for the rich. If I should succeed in saving these boys' lives and do nothing for the progress of the law, I should feel sad, indeed. If I can succeed, my greatest reward and my greatest hope will be that I have done something for the tens of thousands of other boys, for the countless unfortunates who must tread the same road in blind childhood that these poor boys have trod – that I have done something to help human understanding, to temper justice with mercy, to overcome hate with love.

Stanley Baldwin, First Earl Baldwin of Bewdley

1867 – 1947

Three times Prime Minister, in 1923, 1924–9 and 1935–7, Baldwin himself claimed:

I speak not as the man in the street, even, but as a man in the field-path, a much simpler person, steeped in tradition and impervious to new ideas.

In an extract from an address to the Classical Association in 1925, he said:

I remember many years ago standing on the terrace of a beautiful villa near Florence. It was a September evening, and the valley below was transfigured in the long horizontal rays of the declining sun. And then I heard a bell, such a bell as never was on land or sea, a bell whose every vibration found an echo in my innermost heart, I said to my hostess, 'That is the most beautiful bell I have ever heard.' 'Yes,' she replied, 'it is an English bell.' And so it was. For generations its sound had gone out over English fields, giving the hours of work and prayer to English folk from the tower of an English abbey, and then came the Reformation, and some wise Italian bought the bell whose work at home was done and sent it to the Valley of the Arno, where after four centuries it stirred the heart of a wandering Englishman and made him sick for home. Thus the chance word of a Latin inscription, a line in the Anthology, a phrase of Horace or a 'chorus ending of Euripides', plucks at the heartstrings and stirs a thousand memories, memories subconscious and ancestral.

Baldwin looked back with most satisfaction on a speech he made in the House of Commons on 6 March 1925 on the theme of peace in industry.

He refused to support a Conservative Private Member's Bill designed to alter the basis of the trade union political levy since he considered it would embitter relations with the unions. He ended with the words:

For two years past, in the face of great difficulties . . . I have striven to consolidate and to breathe a living force into my great Party . . . I want my Party today to make a gesture to the country [of peace] and to say to them: 'We have our majority; we believe in the justice of the Bill which has been brought in today, but we are going to withdraw our hand, and we are not going to push our political advantage home at a time like this. Suspicion which has prevented stability in Europe is the one poison which is preventing stability at home, and we offer the country today this. We, at any rate, are not going to fire the first shot. We stand for peace. We stand for the removal of suspicion in the country. We want to create an atmosphere, a new atmosphere in a new Parliament for a new age, in which the people can come together . . .'

I know – I am as confident as I can be of anything – that that will be the feeling of all those who sit behind me, and that they will accept the Amendment which I have put down in the spirit in which I have moved it. And I have equal confidence in my fellow-countrymen throughout the whole of Great Britain.

Although I know that there are those who work for different ends from most of us in this House, yet there are many in all ranks and all parties who will re-echo my prayer. 'Give peace in our time, O Lord.'

Sir Oswald Mosley

1896 –

Mosley resigned from the Labour Government in 1930 over the question of unemployment and founded first the short-lived New Party then the British Union of Fascists.

Early in his career Mosley practised the art of public speaking in Parliament, practice of which Churchill said 'he stands in much need'. By the time he made his resignation speech on 28 May 1930 he was a master of his art. After a seventy-minute speech criticizing Government policy on unemployment and outlining his own, he ended:

This nation has to be mobilized and rallied for a tremendous effort, and who can do that except the Government of the day? If that effort is not made we may soon come to crisis, to a real crisis. I do not fear that so much, for this reason, that in a crisis this nation is always at its best. This people knows how to handle a crisis, it cools their heads and steels their nerves. What I fear much more than a sudden crisis is a long, slow, crumbling through the years until we sink to the level of a Spain, a gradual paralysis, beneath which all the vigour and energy of this country will succumb. That is a far more dangerous thing, and far more likely to happen unless some effort is made. If the effort is made, how relatively easily can disaster be averted. You have in this country resources, skilled craftsmen among the workers, design and technique among the technicians, unknown and unequalled in any other country in the world. What a fantastic assumption it is that a nation which within the lifetime of every one has put forth efforts of energy and vigour unequalled in the history of the world, should succumb before an economic situation such as the present. If the situation is to be overcome, if the great powers of this country are to be rallied and mobilized for a great national effort, then the Government and Parliament must give a lead. I beg the Government tonight to give the vital forces of this country the chance that they await. I beg Parliament to give that lead.

Cheering broke out throughout the House and the next day the newspapers were generous in their praise. The *Evening Standard*, for example, called it 'one of the most notable Parliamentary achievements of recent times'.

From 1933 to 1937 Mosley made about 200 speeches a year. At times he made use of drums, orchestra, communal singing and spotlights, but there was no doubt of his own powers. The *Leeds Mercury* reported: 'He must be the sort of orator who could thrill a multitude by declaiming the explanatory notes on an income-tax form.'

Franklin Delano Roosevelt

1882 – 1945

Governor of New York before he became the thirty-second President of the United States in 1932, Roosevelt was a powerful speaker. He won the Presidency in four consecutive elections, and during this long period in office was the first President to broadcast directly to the people.

In 1932, the country was in the thick of unprecedented depression. Roosevelt's first Inaugural Address on 4 March 1933 set out his New Deal programme of reform, and concluded as follows:

If I read the temper of our people correctly, we now realize, as we have never realized before, our interdependence on each other; that we cannot merely take, but we must give as well; that if we are to go forward we must move as a trained and loyal army willing to sacrifice for the good of a common discipline, because, without such discipline, no progress is made, no leadership becomes effective.

We are, I know, ready and willing to submit our lives and property to such discipline because it makes possible a leadership which aims at a larger good.

This I propose to offer, pledging that the larger purposes will bind upon us all as a sacred obligation with a unity of duty hitherto evoked only in time of armed strife.

With this pledge taken, I assume unhesitatingly the leadership of this great army of our people, dedicated to a disciplined attack upon our common problems.

Action in this image and to this end is feasible under the form of government which we have inherited from our ancestors.

Our Constitution is so simple and practical that it is possible always to meet extraordinary needs by changes in emphasis and arrangement without loss of essential form.

That is why our constitutional system has proved itself the most superbly enduring political mechanism the modern world has produced. It has met every stress of vast expansion of territory, of foreign wars, of bitter internal strife, of world relations.

It is to be hoped that the normal balance of executive and legislative authority may be wholly adequate to meet the unprecedented task before us. But it may be that an unprecedented demand and need for undelayed action may call for temporary departure from that normal balance of public procedure.

I am prepared under my constitutional duty to recommend the measures that a stricken nation in the midst of a stricken world may require.

These measures, or such other measures as the Congress may build out of its experience and wisdom, I shall seek, within my constitutional authority, to bring to speedy adoption.

But in the event that the Congress shall fail to take one of these two courses, and in the event that the national emergency is still critical, I shall not evade the clear course of duty that will then confront me.

I shall ask the Congress for the one remaining instrument to meet the crisis – broad executive power to wage a war against the emergency as great as the power that would be given to me if we were in fact invaded by a foreign foe.

For the trust reposed in me I will return the courage and the devotion that befit the time. I can do no less.

We face the arduous days that lie before us in the warm courage of national unity; with the clear consciousness of seeking old and precious moral values; with the clean satisfaction that comes from the stern performance of duty by old and young alike.

We aim at the assurance of a rounded and permanent national life.

We do not distrust the future of essential democracy. The people of the United States have not failed. In their need they have registered a mandate that they want direct, vigorous action.

They have asked for discipline and direction under leadership. They have made me the present instrument of their wishes. In the spirit of the gift I take it.

In this dedication of a nation we humbly ask the blessing of God. May He protect each and every one of us! May He guide me in the days to come!

On 29 December 1940, Roosevelt broadcast an appeal for aid to the Allies fighting Nazi aggression, ending with the words:

But all of our present efforts are not enough. We must have more ships, more guns, more planes – more of everything. And this can be accomplished only if we discard the notion of 'business as usual'. This job cannot be done merely by superimposing on the existing productive facilities the added requirements of the nation for defence.

Our defence efforts must not be blocked by those who fear the future consequences of surplus plant capacity. The possible consequences of failure of our defence efforts are now much more to be feared.

And after the present needs of our defence are past, a proper handling of the country's peacetime needs will require all of the new productive capacity, if not still more.

No pessimistic policy about the future of America shall delay the immediate expansion of those industries essential to defence. We need them.

I want to make it clear that it is the purpose of the nation to build now with all possible speed every machine, every arsenal, every factory that we need to manufacture our defence material. We have the men – the skill – the wealth – and above all, the will.

I am confident that if and when production of consumer or luxury goods in certain industries requires the use of machines and raw materials that are essential for defence purposes, then such production must yield, and will gladly yield, to our primary and compelling purpose.

So I appeal to the owners of plants – to the managers – to the workers – to our own Government employees – to put every ounce of effort into producing these munitions swiftly and without stint. With this appeal I give you the pledge that all of us who are officers of your Government will devote ourselves to the same wholehearted extent to the great task that lies ahead.

As planes and ships and guns and shells are produced, your Government, with its defence experts, can then determine how best to use them to defend this hemisphere. The decision as to how much shall be sent abroad and how much shall remain at home must be made on the basis of our over-all military necessities.

We must be the great arsenal of democracy. For us this is an emergency as serious as war itself. We must apply ourselves to our task with the same resolution, the same sense of urgency, the same spirit of patriotism and sacrifice as we would show were we at war.

We have furnished the British great material support and we will furnish far more in the future.

There will be no 'bottlenecks' in our determination to aid Great Britain. No dictator, no combination of dictators, will weaken that determination by threats of how they will construe that determination.

The British have received invaluable military support from the heroic Greek Army and from the forces of all the Governments in exile. Their strength is growing. It is the strength of men and women who value their freedom more highly than they value their lives.

I believe that the Axis powers are not going to win this war. I base that belief on the latest and best of information.

We have no excuse for defeatism. We have every good reason for hope – hope for peace, yes, and hope for the defence of our civilization and for the building of a better civilization in the future.

I have the profound conviction that the American people are now determined to put forth a mightier effort than they have ever yet made to increase our production of all the implements of defence, to meet the threat to our democratic faith.

As President of the United States, I call for that national effort. I call for it in the name of this nation which we love and honour and which we are privileged and proud to serve. I call upon our people with absolute confidence that our common cause will greatly succeed.

On 8 December 1941 Roosevelt addressed a joint session of Congress requesting a declaration of the existence of a state of war between Japan and the United States.

Yesterday, December 7th, 1941 – a date which will live in infamy – the United States of America was suddenly and deliberately attacked by naval and air forces of the empire of Japan.

The United States was at peace with that nation, and, at the solicitation of Japan, was still in conversation with its Government and its Emperor looking toward the maintenance of peace in the Pacific.

Indeed, one hour after Japanese air squadrons had commenced bombing in the American island of Oahu the Japanese Ambassador to the United States and his colleague delivered to our Secretary of State a formal reply to a recent American message. And, while this reply stated that it seemed useless to continue the existing diplomatic negotiations, it contained no threat or hint of war or of armed attack.

It will be recorded that the distance of Hawaii from Japan makes it obvious that the attack was deliberately planned many days or even weeks ago. During the intervening time the Japanese Government has deliberately sought to deceive the United States by false statements and expressions of hope for continued peace.

The attack yesterday on the Hawaiian Islands has caused severe damage to American naval and military forces. I regret to tell you that very many American lives have been lost. In addition, American ships have been reported torpedoed on the high seas between San Francisco and Honolulu.

Yesterday the Japanese Government also launched an attack against Malaya.

Last night Japanese forces attacked Hong Kong.

Last night Japanese forces attacked Guam.

Last night Japanese forces attacked the Philippine Islands.

Last night the Japanese attacked Wake Island.

And this morning the Japanese attacked Midway Island.

Japan has therefore undertaken a surprise offensive extending throughout the Pacific area. The facts of yesterday and today speak for themselves. The people of the United States have already formed their opinions and well understand the implications to the very life and safety of our nation.

As Commander in Chief of the Army and Navy I have directed that all measures be taken for our defence, that always will our whole nation remember the character of the onslaught against us.

No matter how long it may take us to overcome this premeditated invasion, the American people, in their righteous might, will win through to absolute victory.

I believe that I interpret the will of the Congress and of the people when I assert that we will not only defend ourselves to the uttermost but will make it very certain that this form of treachery shall never again endanger us.

Hostilities exist. There is no blinking at the fact that our people, our territory and our interests are in grave danger.

With confidence in our armed forces, with the unbounding determination of our people, we will gain the inevitable triumph. So help us God.

I ask that the Congress declare that since the unprovoked and dastardly attack by Japan on Sunday, December 7th, 1941, a state of war has existed between the United States and the Japanese Empire.

Harold Macmillan

1894 –

Prime Minister from 1957 to 1963, Macmillan never rated himself highly as an orator. He said in a debate on the Depression in July 1935:

I am afraid it has been said of my contributions to these debates that they are too dry, too academic and too precise; but that is not because either in private or public affairs those who speak most readily and babble most freely necessarily feel most deeply. I am much concerned about the future of this country.

Yet, on 3 February 1960, from the balcony of the House of Assembly in Cape Town, he made one of the most famous speeches of modern British history. It was addressed to both Houses of the South African Parliament and was expected to be a congratulatory speech on the golden wedding of the Union of South Africa. Instead, Macmillan outlined Britain's attitude to South Africa in a changing world:

The most striking of all the impressions I have formed since I left London a month ago is of the strength of this African national consciousness. In different places it may take different forms, but it is happening everywhere. The wind of change is blowing through the continent. Whether we like ot or not, this growth of national consciousness is a political fact. We must all accept it as a fact. Our national policies must take account of it. Of course, you understand this as well as anyone. You are sprung from Europe, the home of nationalism. And here in Africa you have yourselves created a full nation – a new nation. Indeed, in the history of our times yours will be recorded as the first of the African nationalisms . . .

It is the basic principle for our modern Commonwealth that we respect each other's sovereignty in matters of internal policy. At the same time, we must recognize that, in this shrinking world in which we live today, the internal policies of one nation may have effects outside it. We may sometimes be tempted to say to each other, 'Mind your own business'. But in these days I would myself expand the old saying so that it runs, 'Mind your own business, but mind how it affects my business, too.'

Let me be very frank with you, my friends. What governments and parliaments in the United Kingdom have done since the war in according independence to India, Pakistan, Ceylon, Malaya and Ghana, and what they will do for Nigeria and the other countries now nearing independence – all this, though we take full and sole responsibility for it, we do in the belief that it is the only way to establish the future of the Commonwealth and of the free world on sound foundations.

All this, of course, is also of deep and close concern to you, for nothing we do in this small world can be done in a corner or remain hidden. What we do today in West, Central and East Africa becomes known to everyone in the Union, whatever his language, colour or tradition.

Let me assure you in all friendliness that we are well aware of this, and that we have acted and will act with full knowledge of the responsibility we have to you and to all our friends. Nevertheless, I am sure you will agree that in our own areas of responsibility we must each do what we think right. What we think right derives from long experience, both of failure and success in the management of our own affairs.

We have tried to learn and apply the lessons of both. Our judgment of right and wrong and of justice is rooted in the same soil as yours – in Christianity and in the rule of law as the basis of a free society.

This experience of our own explains why it has been our aim, in countries for which we have borne responsibility, not only to raise the material standards of living but to create a society which respects the rights of individuals – a society in which men are given the opportunity to grow to their full stature, and that must in our view include the opportunity to have an increasing share in political power and responsibility; a society in which individual merit, and individual merit alone, is the criterion for man's advancement whether political or economic.

Finally, in countries inhabited by several different races, it has been our aim to find the means by which the community can become more of a community, and fellowship can be fostered between its various parts . . .

It may well be that in trying to do our duty as we see it, we shall sometimes make difficulties for you. If this proves to be so we shall regret it. But I know that even so, you would not ask us to flinch from doing our duty. You, too, will do your duty as you see it.

I am well aware of the peculiar nature of the problems with which you are faced here in the Union of South Africa. I know the differences between your situation and that of most of the other States in Africa . . .

As a fellow member of the Commonwealth, it is our earnest desire to give South Africa our support and encouragement, but I hope you won't mind my saying frankly that there are some aspects of your policies which make it impossible for us to do this without being false to our own deep convictions about the political destinies of free men to which in our own territories we are trying to give effect.

I think we ought as friends to face together – without seeking to apportion credit or blame – the fact that in the world of today this difference of outlook lies between us . . .

———————————

155

Edward VIII

1894 – 1972

Edward VIII spoke well, and, on a tour of the U.S.A. and Canada as
Prince of Wales, a special correspondent of *The Times* reported: 'He has a
happy knack of saying the right thing in the right way, and his clear
boyish voice has a quality of sympathy and sincerity which makes the
speaker one with his audience.'

Inevitably, however, it is his Abdication Speech of 11 December 1936
which is remembered:

At long last I am able to say a few words of my own.

I have never wanted to withhold anything, but until now it has
been not constitutionally possible for me to speak.

A few hours ago I discharged my last duty as King and Emperor,
and now that I have been succeeded by my brother, the Duke of
York, my first words must be to declare my allegiance to him.
This I do with all my heart.

You all know the reasons which have impelled me to renounce
the throne. But I want you to understand that in making up my
mind I did not forget the country or the Empire which as Prince
of Wales, and lately as King, I have for twenty-five years tried to
serve. But you must believe me when I tell you that I have found
it impossible to carry the heavy burden of responsibility and to
discharge my duties as King as I would wish to do without the
help and support of the woman I love.

And I want you to know that the decision I have made has been
mine and mine alone. This was a thing I had to judge entirely for
myself. The other person most concerned has tried up to the last
to persuade me to take a different course. I have made this, the
most serious decision of my life, upon a single thought of what
would in the end be the best for all.

This decision has been made less difficult to me by the sure
knowledge that my brother, with his long training in the public

affairs of this country and with his fine qualities, will be able to take my place forthwith, without interruption or injury to the life and progress of the Empire. And he has one matchless blessing, enjoyed by so many of you and not bestowed on me – a happy home with his wife and children.

During these hard days I have been comforted by my mother and by my family. The Ministers of the Crown, and in particular Mr Baldwin, the Prime Minister, have always treated me with full consideration. There has never been any constitutional difference between me and them and between me and Parliament. Bred in the constitutional tradition by my father, I should never have allowed any such issue to arise.

Ever since I was Prince of Wales, and later on when I occupied the Throne, I have been treated with the greatest kindness by all classes, wherever I have lived or journeyed throughout the Empire. For that I am very grateful.

I now quit altogether public affairs, and I lay down my burden. It may be some time before I return to my native land, but I shall always follow the fortunes of the British race and Empire with profound interest, and if at any time in the future I can be found of service to His Majesty in a private station I shall not fail. And now we all have a new King. I wish him, and you, his people, happiness and prosperity with all my heart. God bless you all. God Save the King.

Neville Chamberlain

1869 – 1940

Neville Chamberlain, Joe Chamberlain's son, was elected a Conservative M.P. in 1918, and was Prime Minister from 1937 to 1940. He believed in his own mission to secure the peace of the world, and, on his return from Munich in September 1938, said to a cheering crowd at Downing Street:

This is the second time that there has come back from Germany to Downing Street peace with honour. I believe it is peace for our time.

George VI

1895 – 1952

George VI never overcame his dislike of public speaking and, indeed, had to undergo periodic treatment to correct a stammer.

He wrote in his diary before making his Christmas broadcast of 1939: 'This is always an ordeal for me and I don't begin to enjoy Christmas until after it is over.'

Nevertheless, he made a number of inspiring speeches, especially during the war.

On 3 September 1939 he broadcast the following speech:

In this grave hour, perhaps the most fateful in our history, I send to every household of my peoples, both at home and overseas, this message, spoken with the same depth of feeling for each one of you as if I were able to cross your threshold and speak to you myself.

For the second time in the lives of most of us we are at war. Over and over again we have tried to find a peaceful way out of the differences between ourselves and those who are now our enemies. But it has been in vain. We have been forced into a conflict. For we are called, with our allies, to meet the challenge of a principle which, if it were to prevail, would be fatal to any civilized order in the world.

At Christmas that year, he ended a speech with the words:

A new year is at hand. We cannot tell what it will bring. If it brings peace, how thankful we shall all be. If it brings us continued struggle, we shall remain undaunted.

In the meantime, I feel that we may all find a message of encouragement in the lines which, in my closing words, I would like to say to you: 'I said to the man who stood at the Gate of the Year, "Give me a light that I may tread safely into the unknown". And he replied, "Go out into the darkness, and put your hand into the Hand of God. That shall be to you better than light, and safer than a known way." '

May that Almighty Hand guide and uphold us all.

General George Smith Patton

1885 – 1945

The great combat leader of the Second World War who swept across Africa, then Sicily, and finally led the Third Army into Germany, Patton was America's most flamboyant general. He believed in plain straight-forward speaking, and in England in May 1944, before the D-Day invasion, made a speech to his troops which they loved, though his officers were uncomfortable about it:

Men, this stuff some sources sling around about America wanting to stay out of the war and not wanting to fight is a lot of balony! Americans love to fight, traditionally. All real Americans love the sting and clash of battle. America loves a winner. America will not tolerate a loser. Americans despise a coward, Americans play to win. That's why America has never lost and never will lose a war.

You are not all going to die. Only two per cent of you, right here today, would be killed in a major battle. Death must not be feared. Death, in time, comes to all of us. And every man is scared in his first action. If he says he's not, he's a Goddam liar. Some men are cowards, yes, but they fight just the same, or get the hell slammed out of them. The real hero is the man who fights even though he's scared. Some get over their fright in a minute under fire, others take an hour, for some it takes days, but a real man will never let the fear of death overpower his honour, his sense of duty, to his country and to his manhood.

All through your Army careers, you've been bitching about what you call 'chicken-shit drill'. That, like everything else in the Army, has a definite purpose. That purpose is Instant Obedience to Orders and to create and maintain Constant Alertness! This must be bred into every soldier. A man must be alert all the time if he expects to stay alive. If not, some German son-of-a-bitch will sneak up behind him with a sock full o' shit! There are four hundred neatly marked graves somewhere in Sicily, all because ONE man went to sleep on his job . . . but they are German graves, because WE caught the bastards asleep! An Army is a team, lives, sleeps, fights, and eats as a team. This individual hero stuff is a lot of horse shit. The bilious bastards who write that kind of stuff for the *Saturday Evening Post* don't know any more about real fighting under fire than they know about fucking!

Every single man in the Army plays a vital role. Every man has his job to do and must do it. What if every truck driver decided that he didn't like the whine of a shell overhead, turned yellow and jumped headlong into a ditch? What if every man thought, 'They won't miss me, just one in millions?' Where in hell would we be now? Where would our country, our loved ones, our homes, even the world, be? No, thank God, Americans don't think like that. Every man does his job, serves the whole. Ordnance men supply and maintain the guns and vast machinery of this war, to keep us rolling. Quartermasters bring up clothes and food, for where we're going there isn't a hell of a lot to steal. Every last man on K.P. has a job to do, even the guy who boils the water to keep us from getting the G.I. shits!

Remember, men, you don't know I'm here. No mention of that is to be made in any letters. The U.S.A. is supposed to be wondering what the hell has happened to me. I'm not supposed to be commanding this Army. I'm not supposed even to be in England. Let the first bastards to find out be the Goddam Germans. I want them to look up and howl, 'Ach, it's the Goddam Third Army and that son-of-a-bitch Patton again!'

We want to get this thing over and get the hell out of here and get at those purple-pissin' Japs!!! The shortest road home is through Berlin and Tokyo! We'll win this war, but we'll win it only by showing the enemy we have more guts than they have or ever will have!

There's one great thing you men can say when it's all over and you're home once more. You can thank God that twenty years from now, when you're sitting around the fireside with your grandson on your knee and he asks you what you did in the war, you won't have to shift him to the other knee, cough, and say, 'I shovelled shit in Louisiana.'

Aneurin Bevan

1897 – 1960

Son of a Welsh miner and himself sent to work down a mine, Bevan rose through local politics to be Labour M.P. for Ebbw Vale in 1929, a seat which he retained until his death. Throughout the war he criticized Churchill for running a one-man government and was rewarded with the epithet 'squalid nuisance'. As Minister of Health and Housing from 1945 to 1951 his greatest achievement was the introduction of the National Health Service. He resigned when Gaitskell proposed to introduce certain charges into the Health Service, and for the remainder of his life he was in opposition.

According to Michael Foot: 'No one who heard him could deny the quality of his artistry. He was the greatest master of the spoken word in British politics in this century, second only, if second at all, to Lloyd George.'

It is difficult to illustrate the quality of his speaking with only a short extract. He thought on his feet continually and disliked grandiloquent rhetoric.

In a speech to the House on 9 February 1948 he condemned the leaders of the British Medical Association for their hostile attitude towards the introduction of the National Health Service. He ended with the words:

If Members opposite think there is anything in the Act which interferes with the freedom of choice, they should say so; we should hear it. If they think there is anything in the Act, scheme, or terms of remuneration, which prejudices the doctor-patient relationship, we should hear it. So far, we have not. We do not object, and never have objected, to the doctors expressing their opinions freely; we do not object to the B.M.A. recommending their doctors not to take service under this scheme. What we do take serious objection to is to organized sabotage of an Act of Parliament. We desire to know from the Opposition whether they support that. Do they support the B.M.A. organizing resistance on 5 July, because I would warn them that the beginning of that road might look very pleasant but the end would be exceedingly unpleasant, not only for us but for Members opposite. [An Hon. Member: Is that a threat?] It must be clear to everybody that if there is one thing we must assert, it is the sovereignty of Parliament over any section of the community. We have not yet made B.M.A. House into another revising Chamber. We have never accepted the position that this House can be dictated to by any section of the community.

We do concur in the right of any section of the community to try to persuade the House of Commons to change its mind. That is perfectly sound. The position we are taking up is that the B.M.A. have exceeded their just constitutional limitations, and that the best thing they can do now is to put on record their opinion that while they may disagree with the Act in this or that particular, or in general if they wish, nevertheless they will loyally accept the decision of Parliament and continue to agitate for such revisions as they think proper. That is the right position for any section of the community to take up.

May I say this in conclusion? I think it is a sad reflection that this great Act, to which every Party has made its contribution, in which every section of the community is vitally interested, should have so stormy a birth. I should have thought, and we all hoped, that the possibilities contained in this Act would have excited the medical profession, that they would have realized that we are setting their feet on a new path entirely, that we ought to take pride in the fact that, despite our financial and economic anxieties, we are still able to do the most civilized thing in the world – put the welfare of the sick in front of every other consideration. I, therefore, deplore the fact that the best elements in the profession have been thrust on one side by the medical politicians, who are not really concerned about the welfare of the people or of their own profession, but are seeking to fish in these troubled waters. I hope the House will not hesitate to tell the British Medical Association that we look forward to this Act starting on 5 July, and that we expect the medical profession to take their proper part in it because we are satisfied that there is nothing in it that any doctor should be otherwise than proud to acknowledge.

In June 1949 at the Labour Party's Blackpool Conference Bevan emphasized the vision behind the Socialist programme of reform:

I would point out that in some way or another the conception of religious dedication must find concrete expression, and I say that never in the history of mankind have the best ideas found more concrete expression than they have in the programme that we are carrying out. 'Suffer the little children to come unto me' is not now something which is said only from the pulpit. We have woven it into the warp and woof of our national life, and we have made the claims of the children come first. What is national planning but an insistence that human beings shall make ethical choices on a national scale? ... The language of priorities is the religion of Socialism. We have accepted over the last four years that the first claim upon the national product shall be decided nationally and they have been those of the women, the children and the old people. What is that except using economic planning in order to serve a moral purpose?

Ernest Bevin

1881 – 1951

Ernest Bevin became a full-time official of the Dockers Union in 1911 and by 1914 was one of the union's three national organizers. In 1922 he was appointed first General Secretary of the new Transport and General Workers Union. He entered the House of Commons in 1940 and served as Minister of Labour and National Service and then as Secretary of State for Foreign Affairs.

According to his biographer and friend, Francis Williams: 'He was not by any standard a great orator but his utterances had a raw strength which compelled conviction. The very clumsiness of his sentences, his contempt for syntax and the niceties of pronunciation, the harshness of his voice and the powerful emphasis of his gestures seemed when he was speaking to a mass audience to make him the embodiment of all natural and unlettered men drawing upon wells of experience unknown to the more literate.'

The Labour Party Conference in October 1950 expressed its alarm at the increasing danger of war and urged measures to improve collective security. The implied criticism of the Labour Government's handling of security provoked Bevin to defend the Government and to urge rejection of the Resolution:

With the support of every member of the Cabinet, I tried from the day I took office until 1947 to be friends with Russia. There is not a speaker who has been on that platform this morning and urged the adoption of this resolution who would stand more insults, more abuse and put up with more than I have put up with from Molotov and Vyshinsky. But I have looked beyond Molotov and Vyshinsky; I have looked for peace, and I have thought, 'I will carry on whatever they say'. I have discussed these problems with Josef Stalin in Moscow. I offered, on behalf of the Government, a fifty years Treaty of Peace. I asked why a little country like Turkey should, for five years, be subjected to a war of nerves. Is Turkey going to attack Russia? Why has she been compelled to stand all the cost of mobilization all this time? She cannot afford it. She is a poor country . . .

Later on in his speech he said:

Foreign policy is a thing that you have got to bring down to its essence as it applies to an individual. It is not something that is great and big; it is common sense and humanity as it applies to my affairs and yours, because it is somebody and somebody's own kindred that are being persecuted and punished and tortured, and they are defenceless. That is a fact. I ask you when you vote on this resolution today to consider: is that what you want?

The resolution was defeated.

———————

Adlai Ewing Stevenson

1900 – 1965

Democratic candidate for President in 1952 and 1956, Stevenson was appointed United States Ambassador to the United Nations by President Kennedy in 1961.

A distinguished speaker, one of his most effective speeches was made on his acceptance of the nomination as Democratic candidate for President on 26 July 1952. After a few introductory remarks he said:

You have summoned me to the highest mission within the gift of any people. I could not be more proud. Better men than I were at hand for this mighty task, and I owe to you and to them every resource of mind and of strength that I possess to make your deed today a good one for our country and for our party. I am confident, too, that your selection of a candidate for Vice-President will strengthen me and our party immeasurably in the hard, the implacable work that now lies ahead of all of us.

I know that you join me in gratitude and in respect for the great Democrats and the leaders of our generation whose names you have considered here in this convention, whose vigour, whose character and devotion to the Republic we love so well have won the respect of countless Americans and enriched our party.

I shall need them, we shall need them, because I have not changed in any respect since yesterday. Your nomination, awesome as I find it, has not enlarged my capacities. So I am profoundly grateful and emboldened by their comradeship and their fealty. And I have been deeply moved by their expressions of good will and support. And I cannot, my friends, resist the urge to take the one opportunity that has been afforded me to pay my humble respects to a very great and good American [Truman's Vice President] whom I am proud to call my kinsman – Alben Barkley of Kentucky.

I hope and pray that we Democrats, win or lose, can campaign not as a crusade to exterminate the opposing party, as our opponents seem to prefer, but as an opportunity to educate and elevate a people whose destiny is leadership, not alone of a rich and prosperous, contented country in the past, but of a world in ferment.

And, my friends, even more important than winning the election is governing the nation. That is the test of a political party – the acid, final test. When the tumult and the shouting die, when the bands are gone and the lights are dimmed, there is the stark reality of responsibility in an hour of history haunted with those gaunt, grim spectres of strife, dissension, and ruthless, inscrutable and hostile power abroad.

The ordeal of the twentieth century – the bloodiest, most turbulent era of the Christian age – is far from over. Sacrifice, patience, understanding, and implacable purpose may be our lot for years to come.

Let's face it. Let's talk sense to the American people. Let's tell them the truth, that there are no gains without pains, that we are now on the eve of great decisions, not easy decisions, like resistance when you're attacked, but a long, patient, costly struggle which alone can assure triumph over the great enemies of man – war, poverty, and tyranny – and the assaults upon human dignity which are the most grievous consequences of each.

Let's tell them that the victory to be won in the twentieth century, this portal to the golden age, mocks the pretensions of individual acumen and ingenuity. For it is a citadel guarded by thick walls of ignorance and mistrust which do not fall before the trumpets' blast or the politicians' imprecations or even the generals' baton. They are, my friends, walls that must be directly stormed by the hosts of courage, morality, and of vision, standing shoulder to shoulder, unafraid of ugly truth, contemptuous of lies, half-truths, circuses, and demagoguery.

Help me to do the job this autumn of conflict and campaign; help me to do the job in these years of darkness, of doubt, and of crisis which stretch beyond the horizon of tonight's happy vision, and we will justify our glorious past and the loyalty of silent millions who look to us for compassion, for understanding, and for honest purpose. Thus we will serve our great tradition greatly.

I ask of you all you have; I will give to you all I have, even as he who came here tonight and honoured me, as he has honoured you

166

– the Democratic party – by a lifetime of service and bravery that will find him an imperishable page in the history of the Republic and of the Democratic party – President Harry S. Truman.

And finally, my friends, in the staggering task that you have assigned me, I shall always try 'to do justly, to love mercy, and walk humbly with God'.

Dwight David Eisenhower

1890 – 1969

The former Supreme Commander of Allied Forces in Western Europe, Eisenhower was elected President in 1952 by a huge majority.

On 8 December 1953 he spoke before the General Assembly of the United Nations suggesting the pooling of atomic materials for peaceful use. In part of it, he said:

I know that the American people share my deep belief that if a danger occurs in the world, it is a danger shared by all – and equally, that if a hope exists in the mind of one nation, that hope should be shared by all.

I feel impelled to speak today in a language that in a sense is new – which I, who have spent so much of my life in the military profession, would have preferred never to use.

That new language is the language of atomic warfare.

Occasional pages of history do record the faces of the 'Great Destroyers' but the whole book of history reveals mankind's never-ending quest for peace and mankind's God-given capacity to build.

It is with the book of history, and not with isolated pages, that the United States will ever wish to be identified. My country wants to be constructive, not destructive. It wants agreements, not wars, among nations. It wants itself to live in freedom and in the confidence that the people of every other nation enjoy equally the right of choosing their own way of life.

So my country's purpose is to help us move out of this dark chamber of horrors into the light, to find a way by which the minds of men, the hope of men, the souls of men everywhere, can move forward toward peace and happiness and well-being.

In this quest I know that we must not lack patience.

I know that in a world divided, such as ours today, salvation cannot be attained by one dramatic act.

I know that many steps will have to be taken over many months before the world can look at itself one day and truly realize that a new climate of mutually peaceful confidence is abroad in the world.

But I know, above all else, that we must start to take these steps – now.

The gravity of the time is such that every new avenue of peace, no matter how dimly discernible, should be explored.

There is at least one new avenue of peace which has not yet been well explored – an avenue now laid out by the General Assembly of the United Nations.

The United States, heeding the suggestion of the General Assembly of the United Nations, is instantly prepared to meet privately with such other countries as may be 'principally involved', to seek 'an acceptable solution' to the atomic armament race which overshadows not only the peace but the very life of the world.

We shall carry into these private or diplomatic talks a new conception.

The United States would seek more than the mere reduction or elimination of atomic materials available for military purposes.

It is not enough just to take this weapon out of the hands of the soldiers. It must be put into the hands of those who will know how to strip its military casing and adapt it to the arts of peace.

The United States knows that if the fearful trend of atomic military build-up can be reversed, this greatest of destructive forces can be developed into a great boon, for the benefit of all mankind.

The United States knows that peaceful power from atomic energy is no dream of the future. That capability, already proved, is here – now – today. Who can doubt, if the entire body of the world's scientists and engineers had adequate amounts of fissionable material with which to test and develop their ideas, that this capability would rapidly be transformed into universal, efficient, and economic usage?

To hasten the day when fear of the atom will begin to disappear from the minds of the people and the governments of the East and West, there are certain steps that can be taken now.

Hugh Gaitskell

1906 – 1963

A former academic, Hugh Gaitskell became Leader of the Parliamentary Labour Party in 1955. At the Labour Party Conference in October that year he expounded his basic political beliefs:

I would like to tell you, if I may, why I am a Socialist and have been for some thirty years. I became a Socialist quite candidly not so much because I was a passionate advocate of public ownership but because at a very early age I came to hate and loathe social injustice, because I disliked the class structure of our society, because I could not tolerate the indefensible difference of status and income which disfigures our society. I hated the insecurity that affected such a large part of our community while others led lives of security and comfort. I became a Socialist because I hated poverty and squalor.

At another Conference, in 1960, he ended a speech on the question of unilateral disarmament with the famous words:

In a few minutes the Conference will make its decision. Most of the votes, I know, are pre-determined and we have been told what is likely to happen. We know how it comes about. I sometimes think, frankly, that the system we have, by which great unions decide their policy before even their conferences can consider the Executive recommendation is not really a very wise one or a good one. Perhaps in a calmer moment this situation could be looked at.

I say this to you: we may lose the vote today and the result may deal this Party a grave blow. It may not be possible to prevent it, but I think there are many of us who will not accept that this blow need be mortal, who will not believe that such an end is inevitable.

There are some of us, Mr Chairman, who will fight and fight and fight again to save the Party we love. We will fight and fight and fight again to bring back sanity and honesty and dignity, so that our Party with its great past may retain its glory and its greatness.

It is in that spirit that I ask delegates who are still free to decide how they vote, to support what I believe to be a realistic policy on defence, which yet could so easily have united the great Party of ours, and to reject what I regard as the suicidal path of unilateral disarmament which will leave our country defenceless and alone.

John Fitzgerald Kennedy
1917 – 1963

In 1960 at the age of forty-three, Kennedy was the youngest man and the first Catholic to be elected President of the United States. His famous Inaugural Address of 20 January 1961 underwent many drafts, and one of his closest aides, Theodore Sorensen, mentioned the suggestions for this speech he received from others, including Galbraith, Dean Rusk, Stevenson, and even Billy Graham, from whom he obtained a list of possible Biblical quotations. Despite this, he described Kennedy as the 'principal architect' of the speech 'however numerous the assistant artisans'.

We observe today not a victory of party but a celebration of freedom, symbolizing an end as well as a beginning, signifying renewal as well as change. For I have sworn before you and Almighty God the same solemn oath our forebears prescribed nearly a century and three-quarters ago.

The world is very different now. For man holds in his mortal hands the power to abolish all forms of human poverty and all forms of human life. And yet the same revolutionary belief for which our forebears fought is still at issue around the globe, the belief that the rights of man come not from the generosity of the state but from the hand of God.

We dare not forget today that we are the heirs of that first revolution. Let the word go forth from this time and place, to friend and foe alike, that the torch has been passed to a new generation of Americans, born in this century, tempered by war, disciplined by a hard and bitter peace, proud of our ancient heritage, and unwilling to witness or permit the slow undoing of those human rights to which this nation has always been committed, and to which we are committed today at home and around the world.

Let every nation know, whether it wishes us well or ill, that we shall pay any price, bear any burden, meet any hardship, support any friend, oppose any foe to assure the survival and the success of liberty.

This much we pledge – and more.

To those old allies whose cultural and spiritual origins we share, we pledge the loyalty of faithful friends. United, there is little we cannot do in a host of co-operative ventures. Divided, there is little we can do, for we dare not meet a powerful challenge at odds and split asunder.

To those new states whom we welcome to the ranks of the free, we pledge our word that one form of colonial control shall not have passed away merely to be replaced by a far more iron tyranny. We shall not always expect to find them supporting our view. But we shall always hope to find them strongly supporting their own freedom, and to remember that, in the past, those who foolishly sought power by riding the back of the tiger ended up inside.

To those peoples in the huts and villages of half the globe struggling to break the bonds of mass misery, we pledge our best efforts to help them help themselves, for whatever period is required, not because the Communists may be doing it, not because we seek their votes, but because it is right. If a free society cannot help the many who are poor, it cannot save the few who are rich.

To our sister republics south of our border, we offer a special pledge: to convert our good words into good deeds, in a new alliance for progress, to assist free man and free governments in casting off the chains of poverty. But this peaceful revolution of hope cannot become the prey of hostile powers. Let all our neighbours know that we shall join with them to oppose aggression or subversion anywhere in the Americas. And let every other power know that this hemisphere intends to remain the master of its own house.

To that world assembly of sovereign states, the United Nations, our last best hope in an age where the instruments of war have far outpaced the instruments of peace, we renew our pledge of support; to prevent it from becoming merely a forum for invective, to strengthen its shield of the new and the weak, and to enlarge the area in which its writ may run.

Finally, to those nations who would make themselves our adversary, we offer not a pledge but a request: that both sides begin anew the quest for peace, before the dark powers of destruction unleashed by science engulf all humanity in planned or accidental self-destruction.

We dare not tempt them with weakness. For only when our arms are sufficient beyond doubt can we be certain beyond doubt that they will never be employed.

But neither can two great and powerful groups of nations take comfort from our present course – both sides overburdened by the cost of modern weapons, both rightly alarmed by the steady spread of the deadly atom, yet both racing to alter that uncertain balance of terror that stays the hand of mankind's final war.

So let us begin anew, remembering on both sides that civility is not a sign of weakness, and sincerity is always subject to proof. Let us never negotiate out of fear, but let us never fear to negotiate.

Let both sides explore what problems unite us instead of belabouring those problems which divide us.

Let both sides, for the first time, formulate serious and precise proposals for the inspection and control of arms, and bring the absolute power to destroy other nations under the absolute control of all nations.

Let both sides seek to invoke the wonders of science instead of its terrors. Together let us explore the stars, conquer the deserts, eradicate disease, tap the ocean depths and encourage the arts and commerce.

Let both sides unite to heed in all corners of the earth the command of Isaiah to 'undo the heavy burdens ... [and] let the oppressed go free'.

And if a beachhead of co-operation may push back the jungle of suspicion, let both sides join in creating a new endeavour, not a new balance of power, but a new world of law, where the strong are just, and the weak secure and the peace preserved.

All this will not be finished in the first one hundred days. Nor will it be finished in the first one thousand days, nor in the life of this Administration, nor even perhaps in our lifetime on this planet. But let us begin.

In your hands, my fellow citizens, more than mine, will rest the final success or failure of our course. Since this country was founded, each generation of Americans has been summoned to give testimony to its national loyalty. The graves of young Americans who answered the call to service surround the globe.

Now the trumpet summons us again – not as a call to bear arms, though arms we need; not as a call to battle, though embattled we are, but a call to bear the burden of a long twilight struggle, year in and year out, 'rejoicing in hope, patient in tribulation', a struggle against the common enemies of man: tyranny, poverty, disease and war itself.

Can we forge against these enemies a grand and global alliance, North and South, East and West, that can assure a more fruitful life for all mankind? Will you join in that historic effort?

In the long history of the world, only a few generations have been granted the role of defending freedom in its hour of maximum danger. I do not shrink from this responsibility; I welcome it. I do not believe that any of us would exchange places with any other people or any other generation. The energy, the faith, the devotion which we bring to this endeavour will light our country and all who serve it, and the glow from that fire can truly light the world.

And so, my fellow Americans, ask not what your country can do for you; ask what you can do for your country.

My fellow citizens of the world, ask not what America will do for you, but what together we can do for the freedom of man.

Finally, whether you are citizens of America or citizens of the world, ask of us here the same high standards of strength and sacrifice which we ask of you. With a good conscience our only sure reward, with history the final judge of our deeds, let us go forth to lead the land we love, asking His blessing and His help, but knowing that here on earth God's work must truly be our own.

Malcolm Little (Malcolm X)

1925 – 1965

The Negro radical Malcolm X was a leading exponent of black nationalist strategy until his assassination in 1965. On 24 March 1961, in the period when he was most deeply involved with the Black Muslims, he made a speech at Harvard in which he said:

But these twenty million black people here in America now number a nation in their own right. Do you believe that a nation within another nation can be successful, especially when they both have equal educations? Once the slave has his master's education, the slave wants to be like his master, wants to share his master's property, and even wants to exercise the same privileges as his master while he is yet in his master's house. This is the core of America's troubles today: there will be no peace for America as long as twenty million so-called Negroes are here begging for the rights which America knows she will never grant us. The limited education America has granted her ex-slaves has even already produced great unrest. Almighty God says the only way for America to ever have any future or prosperity is for her twenty million ex-slaves to be separated from her, and it is for this reason that Mr Muhammad [Black Muslim leader] teaches us that we must have some land of our own. If we receive equal education, how long do you expect us to remain your passive servants, or second-class citizens? There is no such thing as a second-class citizen. We are full citizens, or we are not citizens at all. When you teach a man the science of government, he then wants an equal part or position in that government, or else he wants his own government. He begins to demand equality with his master. No man with education equal to your own will serve you. The only way you can continue to rule us is with superior knowledge, by continuing to withhold equal education from our people. America has not given us equal education, but she has given us enough to make us want more and to make us demand equality of opportunity. And since this is causing unrest plus international embarrassment, the only solution is immediate separation. As your colleges and universities turn out an ever-increasing number of so-called Negro graduates with education equal to yours, they will automatically increase their demands for equality in everything else. Equal education will increase their spirit of equality and make them feel that they should have everything that you have, and their increasing demands will become a perpetual headache for you and continue to cause you international embarrassment. In fact, those Negro students whom you are educating today will soon be demanding the same things you now hear being demanded by Mr Muhammad and the Muslims.

In concluding, I must remind you that your own Christian Bible states that God is coming in the last days or at the end of the old world, and that God's coming will bring about a great separation. Now since we see all sorts of signs throughout the earth that indicate that the time of God's coming is upon us, why don't you repent while there is yet time? Do justice by your faithful ex-slaves. Give us some land of our own right here, some separate states, so we can separate ourselves from you. Then everyone will be satisfied, and perhaps we will all be able to then live happily ever after and, as your own Christian Bible says, 'everyone under his own vine and fig tree'. Otherwise all of you who are sitting here, your Government, and your entire race will be destroyed and removed from this earth by Almighty God, Allah.

Martin Luther King

1929 – 1968

The son of a Baptist minister who was himself one of the pioneers of the Negro resistance movement, Martin Luther King became a renowned minister and Negro leader. His doctrine of passive resistance won him the Nobel Peace Prize in 1964.

King himself thought that his 'greatest talent, strongest tradition, and most constant interest' was not action but 'the eloquent statement of ideas'. On 28 August 1963 at a civil rights demonstration in Washington, in front of 250,000 people, he proclaimed:

I have a dream that my four little children will one day live in a nation where they will not be judged by the colour of their skin but by the content of their character.

I have a dream today.

I have a dream that one day the state of Alabama, whose governor's lips are presently dripping with the words of interposition and nullification, will be transformed into a situation where little black boys and black girls will be able to join hands with little white boys and white girls and walk together as sisters and brothers.

I have a dream today.

I have a dream that one day every valley shall be exalted, every hill and mountain shall be made low, the rough places will be made plain, and the crooked places will be made straight and the glory of the Lord shall be revealed, and all flesh shall see it together.

This is our hope. This is the faith with which I return to the South. With this faith we will be able to hew out of the mountains of despair a stone of hope. With this faith we will be able to transform the jangling discords of our nation into a beautiful symphony of brotherhood. With this faith we will be able to work together, to pray together, to struggle together, to go to jail together, to stand up for freedom together, knowing that we will be free one day.

This will be the day when all of God's children will be able to sing with new meaning 'My country 'tis of thee, sweet land of liberty, of thee I sing. Land where my fathers died, land of the pilgrim's pride, from every mountainside, let freedom ring.'

And if America is to be a great nation this must become true. So let freedom ring from the prodigious hilltops of New Hampshire! Let freedom ring from the mighty mountains of New York! Let freedom ring from the heightening Alleghenies of Pennsylvania!

Let freedom ring from the snowcapped Rockies of Colorado!

Let freedom ring from the curvaceous peaks of California!

But not only that; let freedom ring from Stone Mountain of Georgia!

Let freedom ring from every hill and mole hill of Mississippi. From every mountainside, let freedom ring.

When we let freedom ring, when we let it ring from every village and every hamlet, from every state and every city, we will be able to speed up that day when all of God's children, black men and white men, Jews and Gentiles, Protestants and Catholics, will be able to join hands and sing in the words of that old Negro spiritual, 'Free at last! Free at last! Thank God almighty, we are free at last!'

Robert Kennedy

1925 – 1968

On 5 April 1968, whilst campaigning in Cleveland and only sixty days before his own assassination, Robert Kennedy spoke of the death of Martin Luther King:

This is a time of shame and sorrow. It is not a day for politics. I have saved this one opportunity to speak briefly to you about this mindless menace of violence in America which again stains our land and everyone of our lives.

It is not the concern of any one race. The victims of the violence are black and white, rich and poor, young and old, famous and unknown. They are, most important of all, human beings whom other human beings loved and needed. No one – no matter where he lives or what he does – can be certain who will suffer from some senseless act of bloodshed. And yet it goes on and on.

Why? What has violence ever accomplished? What has it ever created? No martyr's cause has ever been stilled by his assassin's bullet. No wrongs have ever been righted by riots and civil disorders. A sniper is only a coward, not a hero, and an uncontrolled, uncontrollable mob is only the voice of madness, not the voice of the people.

Whenever any American's life is taken by another American unnecessarily – whether it is done in the name of the law or in the defiance of law, by one man or a gang, in cold blood or in passion, in an attack of violence or in response to violence – whenever we tear at the fabric of life which another man has painfully and clumsily woven for himself and his children, the whole nation is degraded.

'Among free men,' said Abraham Lincoln, 'there can be no successful appeal from the ballot to the bullet; and those who take such appeal are sure to lose their cause and pay the costs.' Yet we seemingly tolerate a rising level of violence that ignores our common humanity and our claims to civilization alike. We calmly accept newspaper reports of civilian slaughter in far-off lands. We glorify killing on movie and television screens and call it entertainment. We make it easy for men of all shades of sanity to acquire whatever weapons and ammunition they desire.

Too often we honour swagger and bluster and the wielders of force; too often we excuse those who are willing to build their own lives on the shattered dreams of others. Some Americans who preach nonviolence abroad fail to practice it here at home. Some who accuse others of inciting riots have by their own conduct incited them. Some look for scapegoats, others look for conspiracies, but this much is clear: violence breeds violence, repression brings retaliation, and only a cleaning of our whole society can remove this sickness from our soul.

For there is another kind of violence, slower but just as deadly, destructive as the shot or the bomb in the night. This is the violence of institutions; indifference and inaction and slow decay. This is the violence that afflicts the poor, that poisons relations between men because their skin has different colours. This is a slow destruction of a child by hunger, and schools without books and homes without heat in the winter.

This is the breaking of a man's spirit by denying him the chance to stand as a father and as a man among other men. And this too afflicts us all. I have not come here to propose a set of specific remedies nor is there a single set. For a broad and adequate outline we know what must be done. When you teach a man to hate and fear his brother, when you teach that he is a lesser man because of his colour or his beliefs or the policies he pursues, when you teach that those who differ from you threaten your freedom or your job or your family, then you also learn to confront others not as fellow citizens but as enemies – to be met not with co-operation but with conquest, to be subjugated and mastered.

We learn, at the last, to look at our brothers as aliens, men with whom we share a city, but not a community, men bound to us in common dwelling, but not in common effort. We learn to share only a common fear – only a common desire to retreat from each other – only a common impulse to meet disagreement with force. For all this there are no final answers. Yet we know what we must do. It is to achieve true justice among our fellow citizens. The question is whether we can find in our own midst and in our own hearts that leadership of human purpose that will recognize the terrible truths of our existence.

We must admit the vanity of our false distinctions among men and learn to find our own advancement in the search for the advancement of all. We must admit in ourselves that our own children's future cannot be built on the misfortunes of others. We must recognize that this short life can neither be ennobled or enriched by hatred or revenge. Our lives on this planet are too short and the work to be done too great to let this spirit flourish any longer in our land.

Of course we cannot vanquish it with a programme, nor with a resolution. But we can perhaps remember – even if only for a time – that those who live with us are our brothers, that they share with us the same short movement of life, that they seek – as we do – nothing but the chance to live out their lives in purpose and happiness, winning what satisfaction and fulfilment they can. Surely this bond of common faith, this bond of common goal, can begin to teach us something. Surely we can learn, at least, to look at those around us as fellow men and surely we can begin to work a little harder to bind up the wounds among us and to become in our own hearts brothers and countrymen once again.

Lyndon Baines Johnson

1908 – 1973

He succeeded to the Presidency in November 1963 on Kennedy's assassination and won election himself the following year.

On 31 March 1968, Johnson addressed the nation on the war with Vietnam. He called a halt to the bombing of most of North Vietnam, ending his speech with the words:

One day, my fellow citizens, there will be peace in South-east Asia. It will come because the people of South-east Asia want it – those whose armies are at war tonight; those who, though threatened, have thus far been spared.

Peace will come because Asians were willing to work for it and to sacrifice for it – and to die by the thousands for it.

But let it never be forgotten: peace will come also because America sent her sons to help secure it.

It has not been easy – far from it. During the past four and a half years, it has been my fate and my responsibility to be Commander in Chief. I have lived daily and nightly with the cost of this war. I know the pain that it has inflicted. I know perhaps better than anyone the misgivings it has aroused.

This I believe very deeply. Throughout my entire public career I have followed the personal philosophy that I am a free man, an American, a public servant and a member of my party – in that order – always and only.

For thirty-seven years in the service of our nation, first as a Congressman, as a Senator and as Vice President, and now as your President, I have put the unity of the people first. I have put it ahead of any divisive partisanship. And in these times, as in times before, it is true that a house divided against itself by the spirit of faction, of party, of region, of religion, of race, is a house that cannot stand.

There is division in the American house now. There is divisiveness among us all tonight. And holding the trust that is mine, as President of all the people, I cannot disregard the peril of the progress of the American people and the hope and the prospect of peace for all peoples, so I would ask all Americans whatever their personal interest or concern to guard against divisiveness and all of its ugly consequences.

Fifty-two months and ten days ago, in a moment of tragedy and trauma, the duties of this office fell upon me.

I asked then for your help, and God's, that we might continue America on its course binding our wounds, healing our history, moving forward in new unity, to clear the American agenda and to keep the American commitment for all of our people.

United we have kept that commitment. And united we have enlarged that commitment. And through all time to come I think America will be a stronger nation, a more just society, a land of greater opportunity and fulfilment because of what we have all done together in these years of unparalleled achievement.

Our reward will come in the life of freedom and peace and hope that our children will enjoy through ages ahead.

What we won when all of our people united must not now be lost in suspicion and distrust and selfishness and politics among any of our people. And believing this as I do I have concluded that I should not permit the Presidency to become involved in the partisan divisions that are developing in this political year.

With American sons in the fields far away, with America's future under challenge right here at home, with our hopes and the world's hopes for peace in the balance every day, I do not believe that I should devote an hour or a day of my time to any personal partisan causes or to any duties other than the awesome duties of this office – the Presidency of your country.

Accordingly, I shall not seek, and I will not accept, the nomination of my party for another term as your President. But let men everywhere know, however, that a strong and a confident and a vigilant America stands ready tonight to seek an honourable peace; and stands ready tonight to defend an honoured cause, whatever the price, whatever the burden, whatever the sacrifice that duty may require.

Thank you for listening. Good night and God bless all of you.

Richard Milhous Nixon

1913 –

Thirty-seventh President of the United States, Nixon made his first Inaugural Address on 20 January 1969 which, in retrospect, had its moments of irony:

I ask you to share with me today the majesty of this moment. In the orderly transfer of power, we celebrate the unity that keeps us free.

Each moment in history is a fleeting time, precious and unique. But some stand out as moments of beginning, in which courses are set that shape decades or centuries.

For the first time, because the people of the world want peace and the leaders of the world are afraid of war, the times are on the side of peace.

The greatest honour history can bestow is the title of peacemaker. This honour now beckons America – the chance to help lead the world at last out of the valley of turmoil and on to that high ground of peace that man has dreamed of since the dawn of civilization.

If we succeed, generations to come will say of us now living that we mastered our moment, that we helped make the world safe for mankind.

Standing in this same place a third of a century ago, Franklin Delano Roosevelt addressed the nation ravaged by depression, gripped in fear. He could say in surveying the nation's troubles: 'They concern, thank God, only material things.'

Our crisis today is in reverse.

We find ourselves rich in goods, but ragged in spirit; reaching with magnificent precision for the moon, but falling into raucous discord on earth.

We are caught in war, wanting peace. We're torn by division, wanting unity. We see around us empty lives, wanting fulfilment. We see tasks that need doing, waiting for hands to do them.

To a crisis of the spirit, we need an answer of the spirit.

And to find that answer, we need only to look within ourselves.

As we measure what can be done, we shall promise only what we know we can produce; but as we chart our goals we shall be lifted by our dreams.

No man can be fully free while his neighbour is not. To go forward at all is to go forward together.

This means black and white together, as one nation, not two. The laws have caught up with our conscience. What remains is to give life to what is in the law; to insure at last that as all are born equal in dignity before God, all are born equal in dignity before man.

As we learn to go forward together at home, let us also seek to go forward together with all mankind.

I know that peace does not come through wishing for it – that there is no substitute for days and even years of patient and prolonged diplomacy.

I have taken an oath today in the presence of God and my countrymen. To uphold and defend the Constitution of the United States. And to that oath, I now add this sacred commitment: I shall consecrate my office, my energies and all the wisdom I can summon, to the cause of peace among nations.

Let this message be heard by strong and weak alike.

On 21 July 1969, President Nixon spoke over television to the first astronauts to land on the moon. He said:

Because of what you have done, the heavens have become a part of man's world. And as you talk to us from the Sea of Tranquility it requires us to redouble our efforts to bring peace and tranquility to earth.

For one priceless moment in the whole history of man all the people on this earth are truly one – one in their pride in what you have done and one in our prayers that you will return safely to earth.

James Earl Carter

1924 –

Son of a peanut-farmer from Plains, Georgia, who became thirty-ninth U.S. President at the end of 1976. Jimmy Carter has written 'one does not pursue the Presidency by high oratory but by plain talk, not by talking down to people but simply by talking to people'.

On 1 June 1976 Carter spoke at the dedication of a new wing of the Martin Luther King Hospital in Los Angeles. The *New York Times* described his speech as 'one of the most moving speeches on the American racial dilemma heard in a long time', and noted that 'an almost physical wave of love seemed to pass from the black listeners to Mr Carter'.

The speech ended with these words:

I stand before you a candidate for President, a man whose life has been lifted, as yours have been, by the dream of Martin Luther King.

When I started to run for President, there were those who said I would fail, because I am from the South.

But I thought they were wrong. I thought the South was changing and America was changing. I thought the dream was taking hold.

And I ran for President throughout our nation.

We have won in the South, and we have won in the North, and now we come to the West and we ask your help.

For all our progress, we still live in a land held back by oppression and injustice.

The few who are rich and powerful still make the decisions, and the many who are poor and weak must suffer the consequences. If those in power make mistakes, it is not they or their families who lose their jobs or go on welfare or lack medical care or go to jail.

We still have poverty in the midst of plenty.

We still have far to go. We must give our government back to our people. The road will not be easy.

But we still have the dream, Martin Luther King's dream and

your dream and my dream. The America we long for is still out there, somewhere ahead of us, waiting for us to find her.

I see an America poised not only at the brink of a new century but at the dawn of a new era of honest, compassionate, responsive government.

I see an American government that has turned away from scandals and corruption and official cynicism and finally become as decent as our people.

I see an American with a tax system that does not steal from the poor and give to the rich.

I see an America with a job for every man and woman who can work, and a decent standard of living for those who cannot.

I see an America in which my child and your child and every child receives an education second to none in the world.

I see an American Government that does not spy on its citizens or harass its citizens, but respects your dignity and your privacy and your right to be let alone.

I see an American foreign policy that is firm and consistent and generous, and that once again is a beacon for the hopes of the world.

I see an American President who does not govern by vetoes and negativism, but with vigour and vision and affirmative leadership, a President who is not isolated from our people but feels their pain and shares their dreams and takes his strength from them.

I see an America to which Martin Luther King's dream is our national dream.

I see an America on the move again, united, its wounds healed, its head high, a diverse and vital nation, moving into its third century with confidence and competence and compassion, an America that lives up to the majesty of its Constitution and the simple decency of its people.

This is the America that I see and that I am committed to as I run for President.

I ask your help.

You will always have mine.

List of Orators

188

INDEX

INDEX

194